THE ESTHETICIAN'S GUIDE TO OUTSTANDING ESTHETICS!

Proven Techniques From Today's Industry Icons

Anthology Compiled By:

SHELLEY HANCOCK

Licensed Esthetician Since 1988

Skin Care Center Owner Since 1990

Copyright © 2017 Shelley Hancock

All rights reserved. No part of this book may be reproduced or transmitted in any form or by any means without written permission of the author.

DEDICATION

This book is dedicated to all of my fellow Estheticians that aspire
to bring outstanding esthetics to their clients. We hope to inspire
you with our stories of success and let you know
that all things are possible.

I'd like to thank my husband for being right beside me
and always encouraging me to jump.
Love you!

TABLE OF CONTENTS

Introduction i

Chapter 1 When Opportunity Knocks, Step Through the Door Authored by Shelley Hancock 1

Chapter 2 My Story Authored by Mary Nielsen 9

Chapter 3 Succeed – Oh Yes You Can! Authored by Michele Corley .21

Chapter 4 Insatiable Authored by Lauren Snow 33

Chapter 5 The Role of Microcurrent in Aesthetics Authored by Tina Abnoosi 45

Chapter 6 Advancement in Esthetics Over the Last Three Decades Authored by Michele Phelan 57

Chapter 7 Life Changing Esthetics Authored by Becky Kuehn 69

Chapter 8 How To Build A Successful Skin Care Business The S.M.A.R.T. Way Authored by Beverlee Garb, M.P.A. 79

Chapter 9 The Discovery of the Sea's Most Powerful Antioxidant and the Launch of RéjuvaSea Authored by Frederic Fouassier 89

Chapter 10 The Psychology of Getting Paid Your Worth Authored by Grace Mosgeller 101

Chapter 11 Bringing Nutrition to Skincare Professionals, The Healing Power of Nutrition – My Personal Experience Authored by Ginger Hodulik Downey..113

Chapter 12 Gratitude Authored by Ali Shambayati 123

Chapter 13 Finding, Maintaining and Keeping a "Younger Me" Authored by Isabel Dassinger..135

Chapter 14 Success Begins in The Mind Authored by Malinda McHenry 147

Chapter 15 My Journey - The Way We Do Business Has Changed Authored by Maxine Drake 157

Chapter 16 The Importance of Desire, Dedication, and Support Authored by Terri A. Wojak 167

Chapter 17 Esthetics is a Business Authored by Beth Kenerson 177

Chapter 18 It Is Never Too Late. Authored by Margaret Tomaszewicz 191

Chapter 19 Your Money Mindset and Success Authored by Shelley Hancock 205

Introduction

The Estheticians Guide to Outstanding Esthetics is the first book in a series of Anthology books for the beauty industry. I decided to publish this series because the esthetic industry was in need of information and inspiration from its leaders. These industry leaders are the cream of the crop and were chosen to author a chapter which provides a different way of thinking so that you can begin to think out-of-the-box about ways to achieve outstanding results in your esthetic career and/or spa business.

When I titled this book Outstanding Esthetics, I knew I was raising the bar. Outstanding Esthetics can mean many things but at the end of the day, achieving something that is outstanding takes a lot of time and hard work. Sometimes we don't want to put in the hard work it takes to achieve outstanding results, or we don't know how to get there, or perhaps there are too many obstacles in our way. If you are experiencing this or want to achieve outstanding results, then start reading.

There are a couple of ways to read this book. You can read it cover to cover or pick and choose the chapters that most interest you and read just those. I highly recommend reading every chapter as the stories as so very inspiring. Either way, I know you will walk away with the advice and know-how you need to move your esthetic career in the right direction…forward toward success.

This book is abounding with helpful information. Therefore, I suggest you get out your highlighter, bend down pages, take notes with paper and pen, or on your device to keep track of all your newly found tips and ideas that will shape and change your world. There will be many nuggets you can use; I guarantee that!

What is also great is the support you will find for your career and business so whether you read this book as a reference guide or as a motivational book or both, you will certainly learn what you need to achieve the breakthrough results you desire.

THE ESTHETICIAN'S GUIDE TO OUTSTANDING ESTHETICS!

I know myself, and the authors of the Outstanding Esthetics book welcome your thoughts and comments. I urge you to reach out to that specific author who really made you think or provided you with new information. Send an email to let them know your thoughts or provide some comments. I know all of us will appreciate your insights as to what moved you, changed you, and got you to the results you deserve.

Thank you for letting us help you on your results-oriented journey to greater success in the world of esthetics.

Shelley Hancock

Chapter 1

When Opportunity Knocks, Step Through the Door

Authored by Shelley Hancock

On a Tuesday evening at 6 PM in the early months of 1990, I received the phone call that would change my life. It was a woman who owned a skin care center in town. She proceeded to tell me she had the opportunity to become the manager of a resort opening up in another state and she needed someone to run her skin care business. She wanted that someone to be me. I was speechless for a few moments because this was not a phone call I could ever have imagined receiving. The first thoughts that went through my mind were, why me? Was it really me she meant to call?

Let me give you a little background. When this opportunity presented itself, I was just 29 years old and had only been a licensed Esthetician for 18 months. When I graduated esthetic school, I went straight to work in a dermatology office, so I had no experience in the spa atmosphere, and I had absolutely no business background. Not a single college course, no experience whatsoever. Still, this woman chose me to watch over her business. Years later I would understand that she saw something in me I didn't know about myself yet.

She needed an answer the following morning because she was booked on a flight later that afternoon. This was a big decision to make, and I only had 14 hours to make it. I had some heavy thinking to do, and needless to say, I did not sleep a wink that night.

My mind raced back and forth between the position at the dermatology office I had secured with hard work or the opportunity to run a business. Safety or the unknown. Stay with the status quo or venture out to bigger possibilities.

After a long restless night, I decided this was an opportunity that doesn't just drop in one's lap easily, and I couldn't let fear keep me from jumping in with both feet. I decided I was up for the challenge, ready for the adventure. She and I met at her spa the next morning for three hours to go over as much about the business as we could in just three hours. She showed me her bookkeeping program, client information, scheduling system and where everything was in the treatment rooms. Then she left, and I never saw her again.

The next morning when I arrived at the center, I realized the magnitude of what I had just taken on. Here I sat with a skin care business and absolutely no experience on how to run it. The only thing I had going for me was plenty of passion. I was so excited about this new adventure. I felt like a kid the night before Christmas. I don't recall ever feeling any fear, just excitement and that was probably my saving grace.

It wouldn't be until many years later I learned about the Law of Attraction. How what you think about comes about. Where you put your thoughts and what words you use is where your life will go. Well, all I ever thought about and talked about back then was how awesome it was to have this opportunity and how excited I was to build a successful esthetic business. Failure never even entered my mind. All these years later, I truly believe this is why I grew a very successful business. It certainly wasn't from having experience because I barely knew how to be a good esthetician let alone a good business owner.

As I took over this skin care business, I realized why she wanted to leave. It was not a booming business. My first week there I had only three clients. Even being so very slow, I would arrive at the spa every morning at 9 AM whether I had a client or not. I wanted to be there just in case the phone rang. I wanted to be there just in case someone happened to drop by. I dusted, and I rearranged and made it feel like mine. It was my way of telling the universe I was open for business! I am going to be successful.

When I did have a client, and they asked me how things were going, my answer was always "fabulous; I'm super busy, and I couldn't be happier." I said this even if it was Thursday and they were my first client that week. I always spoke, "as if." I never told it like it was. (Only tell it like it is if you like it like it is.) I wanted to be busier, so I spoke as if I was busier and guess what? Fairly quickly, I was busier!

Three months later I called the owner and asked if she was coming back. She wasn't. So, we began negotiating for me to purchase the business and two weeks later I became a business owner. Had I let fear take over when I first received her call I wouldn't be where I am today in my career. This business grew to be extremely successful, and I sold it in 2005 to start a new adventure mentoring my fellow estheticians.

Even with little experience as an esthetician and no experience as a business owner, I used my extreme passion for making it through. We can always find people to help us with what we don't know, but the passion has to come from within, and that can't be purchased.

In March of 2015, another opportunity for an adventure dropped into my lap and once again I jumped. I received a phone message from a company that wanted to chat with me about being a radio show host. I deleted the message; I thought I was being punked!

A week later they called again, and this time I picked up the phone. The first thing out of my mouth again was, "why me?" I was speaking with the executive producer, and he told me they have a staff that combs the internet watching videos. When they come across someone with a personality that would draw people in, and this person seems to be able to speak about numerous things, then they contact that person. They saw my YouTube videos and contacted me.

Once again I was speechless. Another incredible opportunity I could never have imagined was about to drop into my lap. The executive producer proceeded to interview me, and by the end of the call, I was about to become a radio show host. The next week I started my training, and my first show was scheduled for eight weeks out. It was all very overwhelming, but that excitement and passion kicked in to help me through. It wasn't until the week before my first show that a little fear reared its ugly head. What am I doing? Me a radio show host? Seriously Shelley? My executive producer talked me off the ledge, and the first show went smoothly, sweaty palms and all. Within a couple of months, my weekly radio show became fun. The nerves settled down, and I began to enjoy myself.

I get emails every day thanking me for the information I share, and some extremely interesting people have come into my life because of the show. Had I not jumped at this opportunity, our paths would never have crossed.

I wanted to share these two experiences with you in hopes that you may do the same one day when you are faced with an opportunity that looks overwhelming. Instead of letting fear hold you back, jump in with both feet and see where life takes you. My guess is that it will be places you could never have imagined and your life will be more fulfilled because of it. Step out. Be bold. Ignite your passion and go for it.

About Shelley Hancock

Shelley Hancock, (a.k.a 'The Gadget Gal'), is one of the most trusted esthetic advisors of our time and Founder of Shelley Hancock Consulting, an organization dedicated to helping estheticians increase their profits. After owning a successful skin care center for 29 years, Hancock expanded her focus so she could provide a deeper level of service to fellow estheticians. Through hands-on training, workshops and private consultations, she has now connected 1000s of beauty business owners with esthetic equipment that attracts a higher level client and helps build a more successful practice. "Most retailers think the relationship ends with purchase," explains Hancock. "I view it as just the beginning".

When she's not teaching, training, coaching or working with clients, you will find her recording her radio program for Voice America.

Contact Shelley Today!

Website: http://www.ShelleyHancock.com

Email: contactme@shelleyhancock.com

Chapter 2

My Story

Authored by Mary Nielsen

My career into esthetics and entrepreneurship happened because I'm a late bloomer. I'm also Scandinavian. My people are Vikings! Strong, stubborn, and not afraid of adventure. We also believe in a world full of abundance.

Adventure, Appreciation, and Abundance has become my song.

I was working as a nurse in a small town for a multi-specialty surgical practice. Two of the physicians in the group were plastic surgeons. They asked me to investigate what it would take to bring lasers into the practice. This was 1999. I began doing the research, and little angels began whispering in my ear, "You want to do this." I was absolutely fascinated with the technology. My physicians were kind enough to let me take a short leave of absence to attend esthetics school. I have a deep appreciation for their generosity, and I benefitted from their abundance. I became a licensed esthetician. My education adventure was just beginning.

In the late 1990's and early 2000's, the information available to new estheticians was disappointingly limited. My basic esthetics education had been a let-down. The internet had a cumbersome dial-up connection, and few resources had websites. Those that did had little to offer. I scoured the few journals I could find, read every book in the library and ordered more from the advertisements in magazines and journals. I attended several conventions and shows. There were a few esthetician mentors, like Shelley Hancock, who were leaders in the industry. All the while, I was working and learning by trial and error.

The esthetics business of the plastic surgery practice where I was working grew to two locations and was considered a success. I was performing light energy treatments like hair removal, photofacials, skin rejuvenation, and vascular treatments as well as chemical peels, microdermabrasion, and some facials. I began a collaboration with the local cancer center performing facials on oncology clients, with medical approval, just as a way of giving back to the community. This was long before the oncology esthetics term was trademarked by Morag Currin. Becky Kuehn's Oncology Spa Solutions is an industry essential for today's esthetician.

After working for the surgical group for five years, I was presented with an opportunity to open my own skin and laser practice. Flourish Skin & Laser was a labor of love. I felt excited by the adventure and was challenged with the learning curve of business ownership, as well as being the technician performing the treatments. I continued to do the same treatments that I had been doing with the surgical practice but over a ten-year span added body contouring with cryolipolysis and microneedling to the list of treatments. Flourish also had a very healthy retail skin care business.

I also began providing some contracted training services for a laser company. I traveled to clinics across western Canada and the Pacific Northwest providing laser training on my days off at the clinic.

There were some lean times with the economic downturn in 2008, but I was again blessed with abundance as the creditors allowed me to make payments when the revenue fell short. The economy began to turn. Life was humming along; the business was making money. A Small Business Administration loan consolidated debt and eliminated cash flow squeezes. My children were grown, I had grandkids, great friends, and a good life.

And then, Boom! I fell in love. In a several-year courtship that eventually led to relocation and marriage, I sold my business of ten years. After having the freedom of owning my own business for so long, I couldn't imagine going to work for someone. In evaluating my new surroundings, I realized I didn't have it in me to open a new skin and laser clinic in a larger city where no one knew me. I also saw that states were moving toward a second tier of licensure for estheticians to operate advanced devices. I felt confident that my time spent traveling to train staff in clinics could be flipped around and new laser users would travel to my location for the training.

Spectrum Advanced Aesthetics Institute was born. It had its start in a small office space and within three years has tripled in size. We began by offering advanced training to Oregon estheticians who desire the certified advanced esthetician license.

My own basic esthetics training fifteen years before had fallen short. My instructor had just graduated from the class before me and had no life experience to bring depth to the education. He was young and immature. The program was constantly plagued with shortages in rudimentary supplies. It was hair- and nail-focused and very evident that esthetics was an afterthought.

With Spectrum offering training toward advanced licensure, I was faced time and time again with students who hadn't receive a strong, basic esthetics education. I decided to add a basic esthetics program to provide an education geared toward the skills needed to be successful in an advanced certification, or medical esthetics.

I love, love, love what I do. I love coming to work every day. I have an amazing team of people who are working alongside me, carrying on the vision of elevating the profession of esthetics. It is rewarding to see the light bulb turn on when a student grasps complicated theory and concepts. Because I love what I do and my mind is constantly humming along with ways to make things better, I started two additional companies, Cascade Aesthetic Alliance, an organization dedicated to aesthetic professional networking and education, and Skintelligent Resources, a company offering supplemental educational material for esthetic schools.

I came into advanced esthetics intrigued with the technology and a desire to understand laser theory and its interaction with the skin, so the impact of what estheticians really do hit me HARD early on. One of my very first clients was a young attorney. He arrived at his appointment in full suit and tie. He explained that he wanted laser hair removal. He said he was a hairy guy and his body hair was constantly getting tugged by his clothing during the day. He wanted to eliminate that discomfort. "Of course," I assured him. "I need you to take off your shirt so I can make an assessment." While I began completing his consultation form, he removed his tie, jacket, and shirt. I looked up. He was standing in front of me, and he looked like he was wearing a sweater. He had thick dark chest and back hair. A sweater. Really. Ok, maybe a vest. And as I made eye contact with him, his arms fell to his sides. He looked at me and said, "I just want my wife to touch me. She never really hugs me. She might touch the sides of my body where I don't have a lot of body hair, but she never fully embraces me." We completed a series of hair removal over the next year. We never discussed his remarks at his consultation appointment in subsequent sessions. He left after his last appointment, and I thought that would be the last of it. He'd had a significant reduction. About a year later, he popped into the office unannounced, and said, "I just stopped in to thank you. You saved my marriage."

The work we do is more than just buff and puff. We change lives. We impact self-esteem. We impact confidence and self-image. We have the power to influence change.

A second important lesson for any esthy entrepreneur is to give back. Be generous. I believe in the words of Mr. Rogers, "We live in a world in which we need to share responsibility. It's easy to say it's not my child, it's not my community, it's not my world, it's not my problem. Then there are those who see the need and respond. Those people are my heroes." Because we are a part of the human race, we need to share the good juju of our abundance with those who have less. We should not have an expectation of a return. No free marketing, no other intent other than making life better for our fellow human beings. Early in my esthetics career, I began working with the oncology center in town because it seemed like the right thing to do. Spectrum has held diaper drives for community drop-in centers, fulfilled Christmas lists for children at homeless shelters, held dog food drives for pet shelters. None of these efforts were done with the intent of anything more than fulfilling a responsibility to give back. We live in the most abundant country in the world; we are immensely blessed, and our obligation is to reflect that blessing with generosity and abundance.

Consider serving a term on your state board. You can help

influence governmental policies and influence a generation of esthys with your service.

Thirdly, make lifelong learning a priority. We are in an industry that is experiencing double-digit growth. New technology in treatments, equipment, and skin care products, as well as upgrades to best business practices, are being introduced annually. This makes our field exciting. Stay on top of the new trends. Read journals. Search out credible sources on the internet for accurate information. Attend a convention. Join a networking organization. Don't get into a rut.

The fourth tip, don't practice illegally. Every state is different. Educational requirements change state to state along with scope of practice definitions. What may be legal in one state may not be legal in another. It doesn't always make sense. Nonetheless, it's real. Find out from your state board what is legal in your state, and don't try to do differently.

The fifth tip for entrepreneurs is to take a lesson from me. Hire someone to do your bookkeeping. It's well worth the expense to have someone who has expertise in finances help you manage your money. I wasn't willing to spend the money to pay payroll and figure quarterly taxes until the IRS determined my calculations weren't matching their calculations. A payment plan was then implemented, and a payroll service and bookkeeper were retained.

Lastly and probably my most important word of advice: Reassess your life-work balance often. When you are passionate about your career and feel called to do it, it's easy for the hours to become occupied, and your family and friends take a back seat, as well as your own needs. You won't be disappointed spending more time with your family or scheduling your mammogram. Stay well-rounded.

Embrace adventure, appreciation, and abundance in your own journey. You won't regret it.

About Mary Nielsen

A technician, educator, mentor and business owner, Mary Nielsen has been at the forefront of the developments in medical esthetics since its infancy in the early 1990s. A nurse by training and experience, Mary was drawn into advanced medical esthetics with the advent of laser technologies and their use while working for a plastic surgeon. She went on to found her own successful skin and laser clinic. She is currently Vice Chair and Industry Expert on the Oregon Board of Certified Advanced Estheticians. She is the author of the advanced aesthetic textbook, A Compendium for Advanced Aesthetics, a Guide for the Master Esthetician, four books on medical spa policies and procedures, and safety policy and procedures as well as several articles on specific treatments in Skin Inc and Day Spa magazine. She is a contributor to Milady Standard Esthetics: Fundamentals, Edition 12 and writes regularly for Milady Pro.

She is the Executive Director of Spectrum Advanced Aesthetics, founder of Cascade Aesthetic Alliance, Educational Catalyst for Skintelligent Resources, and owner of Indie Aesthetics.

Contact Mary Today!

Email: mary@spectrumlasertraining.com

Chapter 3

Succeed – Oh Yes You Can!

Authored by Michele Corley

When we look up "success" in the dictionary, it reads something like this: the attainment of wealth, position, honors, or the like.

No matter where you grew up, how old you are, what your profession is, or where you are on the socioeconomic scale, most of us want to reach some level of success in life, but to each of us, success will be defined differently.

Success should be defined by you, specific to you and your aspirations. Success to some may mean copious quantities of money, a successful business, or to be a good employer. Success to others may mean being a good employee, spouse, parent or friend. For others, it may be to live a balanced life or leave behind a legacy of good. It could be a combination of many of these things.

What do you truly want from your life? Your success begins with a clearly defined vision, followed by goal setting. Focus and commitment, a positive attitude, perseverance and persistence, and hard work are instrumental in achieving your vision and goals.

Setting aside one's fear of failure and learning from our failures/nonsuccess will provide the learning lessons critical to achieving success. Don't undervalue the wisdom we can receive by listening and learning to those who have come before us. Without these components, you will not be able to overcome the obstacles you will face that will help you become your best self!

Clearly Defined Vision

A clearly defined vision happens when you hone in and specifically define what success looks like for you. By writing down what success looks like you are well on the way to achieving your personalized vision of success. You could have a vision of success for your profession or vocation, family life, health, personal time, how you contribute to society or your community, etc., or any combination of these. Once you have written down your visions, then you begin setting your goals.

Goals

Goals get you from point A (where you are now) to point B (where you want to be). Goal setting should be specific, measurable, achievable, and have a timeline. Goals can be long term, short term, or intermediate. Like your visions goals should be written. Goals should be reviewed in an appropriate time frame, to evaluate your progress and adjust accordingly.

Focus & Commitment

To ensure reaching your goals, stay focused on them; keep them ever present. Post them in your daily planner, or on your bathroom mirror, your computer at work, wherever will work best for you. With focus, disruptions are kept to a minimum and your days are spent in a meaningful way. Focus should be tenacious and determined and ensures you won't let go until the task is accomplished. Remove unnecessary distractions from your life that are consuming energy and preventing you from reaching your goals.

Commitment involves dedicating your time and energy to the pursuit of your visions and goals. Being committed to your goals means taking actions required to reach your goals regardless of circumstances. The choices you make every day need to lead to the result you want. For example, you must stay committed to ideas or actions even during times of doubt, dispassion, and difficulty. Without commitment, your goals will not be achieved.

Balance your focus and commitment, so you are not overly focused on one goal at the expense of others, but without over-committing to too many goals at once. It takes time to find this balance, and the regular review of goals is the time through which you adjust for what life brings, then refocus and recommit to your goals appropriately.

Positive Attitude

A positive attitude is a must if you want to reach your goals. A positive attitude helps you cope more easily with the daily bumps we encounter in life. It brings optimism into life and makes it easier to avoid doubts and unproductive thinking. If you adopt it as a way of life, it will bring constructive changes into your life, and makes achieving success more probable.

It is critical to stop negative thoughts in their path and change them to positive thoughts. As an example, a negative thought, "I'm not going to get any better at this," can be turned into a positive thought, "I'll give it another try. I am sure I can do it."

There are numerous techniques to help you maintain a positive attitude: engage in positive self-talk, positive affirmations, listen to speakers that focus on positive mental attitude, commit to consistent physical exercise, establish a support network, develop an attitude of gratitude and listen to uplifting music.

Perseverance & Persistence

Perseverance is defined as "continued effort to do or achieve something despite difficulties, failure, or opposition." It is essential to recognize that when you are striving towards a goal, it is unlikely you will accomplish it on your first attempt. Perseverance means you decide every day not to give up. Struggle builds character and is a normal step in growth and progress. Take stock of your learning lessons, reevaluate as needed, and move forward never losing sight of your goal. Navigating your way through, around, over or under the obstacles you will encounter will be a reality in achieving goals.

Persistence, persistence, persistence! Never give up. Never let anyone else make you doubt whether you can achieve your goals. Your success is in your own hands. Reach out and take it!

The words of Calvin Coolidge famously known as Press On capture the essence of persistence:

"Nothing in this world can take the place of persistence. Talent will not; nothing is more common than unsuccessful people with talent. Genius will not; unrewarded genius is almost a proverb. Education will not; the world is full of educated derelicts. Persistence and determination alone are omnipotent. The slogan "press on" has solved and always will solve the problems of the human race." – Calvin Coolidge

Work

There is no way around it. You must be willing to put in the necessary work to achieve your goals. It is crucial you push yourself to do the work even when you may not want to, and advantageous to practice at your work until you are good if not great! Success is failure kicked to bits by hard work.

Overcoming Fear of Failure

Have more faith than fear. Reorient your view of failure to a learning lesson. All eventual success stories have experienced countless learning lessons. Remember the only reason you hear a success story is that those individuals involved persevered through the lessons encountered. Learn to be okay with being uncomfortable. The more failures you face and conquer, the more you will cultivate success and self-confidence.

Listen and Learn

Ask relevant and enlightening questions in the areas you want to achieve success and listen to the answers you receive. It is beneficial to slow down and take the time to listen and learn from those individuals you respect and who have reached a high level of expertise in your field. Surround yourself with people you want to be like, watch and learn from them. What did they do right? What can you learn from their experiences? Listening is imperative, and that includes listening to your elders, mentors, customers and last, but not least, yourself.

Conclusion

A favorite story of success, goal setting, commitment, focus, perseverance, persistence, positive attitude and hard work comes from an interview with Thomas Edison. After struggling to develop a viable, electric light bulb for months and months, Thomas Edison was interviewed by a young reporter who boldly asked Mr. Edison if he felt like a failure and if he thought he should just give up by now. Perplexed, Edison replied, "Young man, why would I feel like a failure? And why would I ever give up? I now know definitively over 9,000 ways that an electric light bulb will not work. Success is almost in my grasp." And shortly after that, and over 10,000 attempts, Edison invented the light bulb.

Edison defined success as creating the electric light bulb, and then he reset his goals and moved on to more inventions that would change the world further. The beauty of success is that it can have many layers and it will likely change as we achieve and grow.

Envision your own success, make it personal to your ambitions and aspirations and don't limit your vision to one facet of your life — it can be in as many facets as you desire.

The critical part of achieving success is to define what you want, write it down, reflect daily on the steps that are necessary to write your own story of success. Pursue your goals with focus and commitment, a positive attitude, perseverance and persistence, and hard work. Set aside any fear of failure and learn from your nonsuccess and from those around you!

Succeed. You can and you will. Go for it and never give up!

About Michele Corley

Michele Corley is the founder and President of Michele Corley Clinical Skin Care a nationally distributed professional use only skin care line based in Napa, California. Michele holds a bachelor's degree in business from Georgia Southern University; is a licensed Esthetician; and completed Advanced Cosmetic Chemistry at UCLA. Prior to founding and launching Michele Corley Clinical Skin Care, she earned multiple sales awards while working for a leading skincare contract manufacturer and ranked as a top sales and marketing professional in both the skincare and wine industries. Michele's philosophy is simple: provide efficacious products at reasonable prices and back it up with exceptional customer service. Every Michele Corley Clinical Skin Care product is crafted with care and consideration to the health and well-being of the skin. Michele believes in treating her clients' success as important as her own, and values a true partnership with everyone she has the pleasure to work with.

Contact Michele Today!

Office: 707-637-4996
Email: Info@MicheleCorley.com
Website: http://www.MicheleCorleyClinicalSkinCare.com

Chapter 4

Insatiable

Authored by Lauren Snow

It's strange how a series of chance turns in the road of life can take you to places you never once expected, yet, at the same time, you know you're exactly where you're supposed to be. Twenty years ago if you had asked me if I thought I'd be an esthetician and working in the skin care industry, I would have said, "What's that?" and brushed it off. I always pictured my path in life as a direct line, simply connecting the dots as I went, climbing my way up a corporate ladder of some magical Fortune 500 company. Well, my path didn't include a straight line, much less a line at all. It didn't even include a corporate career in a concrete jungle. My path has been a series of turns; making choices and taking chances, all leading me to where I am today. My story is jagged, it's a little rocky, but it's all mine—and it's real.

I wish I were sharing my magical formula for success with you that morphed me into the executive director of Associated Skin Care Professionals. But there isn't such a thing. I just have three traits that I am certain to have contributed to my success, and those I share with you in this chapter. My career path hasn't exactly been deliberate, but because I am a product of hard work, insatiable curiosity, and leadership, I am where I am today.

GO THE EXTRA MILE—IT'S NEVER CROWDED

If being successful was easy, everyone would do it. It takes hard work. Sometimes it's the work that no one else wants to do, most times it's the work that no one sees you doing. The extra effort of hard work on days when you don't even want to be at work at all is the extra effort that sets you apart and fuels your success. Remember that.

I'm not perfect, and I will be the first to admit I don't have a genius IQ, but I do have a strong work ethic. I have learned you don't have to be the very best at every single thing you do, but you do have to be willing to be the hardest worker. It requires zero talent, but a high level of effort. It's not glamorous, it's not always fun, but the rewards you will reap are tenfold.

Go to work every day with a can-do attitude. Dive in. Get involved. If you're not with a client, keep yourself busy by positively contributing to the spa in whatever way is needed. I am proof that my success is a direct result of being someone who wanted more, had a lot to prove and was willing to put in more work to get there.

HUNGRY FOR MORE

I've always wanted to be somebody that helps change lives. When I was younger, I wanted to be a nurse, a veterinarian, and a teacher. As my world grew, I wanted to be a journalist, a lawyer, and president. Likely similar to your own story, I've held an innate desire to help others my entire life. I've known that I could do this in many capacities, and when I decided to pursue a career in skin care, I thought I'd be changing lives by treating acne and boosting the confidence of my clients. I envisioned myself making them feel more beautiful through the power of human touch and connection. As this goal conceptualized, my desire for more evolved. I realized I could take my talents and aspirations to help others even further by helping estheticians to serve their clients better.

When I first started at ASCP, I worked in the membership department. I worked hard; I wasn't afraid to stay late or jump in head first when they needed me. I got to know the company, member needs and tried to find ways I could help make a difference in the members' experience and my business's processes. As time went on, I was promoted to a program coordinator role where I was able to get involved in improving member benefits more formally, but I didn't stop there. I continued to think freshly, ask questions and make myself invaluable to my team as the director of membership and brand manager.

As I have continued to form my own career path, one theme has remained the same. I get to help people and make a difference in their lives, and that is what has fueled me to keep climbing. My role at ASCP has always been fundamentally about service. Every day I get to serve nearly 17,000 estheticians and make decisions that will positively affect their ability to reach financial stability sooner by protecting their careers and making more money.

PUTTING IN THE WORK

Throughout my career, I've taken positions that got my foot in the door knowing I ultimately wanted a more involved role within the company, as I did with ASCP. Instead of choosing a job, choose the company. It has proven to be a successful strategy because if you're willing to put in the work to get to where you want to be, it doesn't matter where you start. When you become a valuable team player in any role, you are afforded more opportunities to grow. As you continue to grow and can fill many roles, you become invaluable to the company. In esthetics, that may mean taking a job right out of school as a receptionist for the busy spa you want to be a part of. Even if your goal is to become a busy esthetician ultimately, and a receptionist job is all that's open, take it. Use the opportunity to learn the ropes, grow from the experience, and become a valuable asset to the team.

INSATIABLE CURIOSITY

I consider myself a student of life. I can openly admit I don't know everything there is to know about esthetics, and in fact, I love that I don't. I enjoy learning. If something piques my interest, I pursue it. I have an intense hunger for knowledge and an insatiable thirst for answers. Whether that's getting to know an interesting person, learning new skills, or understanding how something works, if there's something I want to know more about, I go and get it. As estheticians, we have so many resources available to us. Whether that's textbooks, online forums, or web searches, we literally have answers at our fingertips. Despite today's technology, don't forget how valuable your peers and mentors can be, too.

I encourage you to ask tough questions. Research different schools of thought. Explore other philosophies. Seek opportunities that push you outside your comfort zone. There is not one person on this planet that knows everything, and when you consider yourself a student of life, you will broaden your scope of knowledge, and it will allow you to embrace being a work in progress, rather than reluctant to admit you don't know it all. Just when you think you know everything about cosmetic chemistry, reach for more. There is always something more to learn.

LEADERS EMPOWER OTHERS

And don't forget to pass that knowledge on to others. Leaders are those that inspire people. Leaders are those that initiate change. You can lead without a leadership title, and you should. Much of getting ahead in the workplace is by rolling up your sleeves, not being afraid to take chances, and by getting things done. Don't wait for someone to tell you what to do if you see something that needs to be done, handle it. If someone in your spa could use your help, jump in. When the work is done, the success will come. We need more leaders in the esthetics industry, and I encourage you to step up and get involved however you feel compelled.

When stepping up as a leader, there is one thing I must caution you to take in stride. You must learn to be ok with being called bossy. I learned at an early age that women who display leadership qualities aren't always called leaders. They can be called overbearing, bossy and whiny. Instead of letting that suppress you, own it. Don't think of it as a derogatory term. Take it as a compliment and let it propel you to continue earning a seat at the table.

We'd be having this discussion over champagne on my own mega-yacht if I had a dollar for every time someone told me I was bossy, whiny or overbearing for speaking up. I would probably have two mega-yachts if I could say I never let other people's opinions get to me. But the truth is, we've all been hurt by the words of others at some point. Don't let them hold you back. Use them to fuel your desire to make a difference.

PROVING MYSELF, TO MYSELF

While I grew up with many strong influences around me, I also grew up with someone who doubted my abilities. This person told me I wasn't enough; not pretty enough, not smart enough, not good enough. This person was me.

I realize I am a work in progress. I've learned to use the negative self-talk and doubt as a conduit for change and momentum, but it wasn't easy. It's something I work on every day. Personal empowerment and the ascent to success is not a static thing you do once in your lifetime and ride the coattails until retirement. It's not a once-you've-got-it-you-can-stop-trying type of passage. It is a self-led journey you must continue to pursue in order to remain sharp, confident and committed to your success. My mantra is: the more you learn, the more you earn.

We have to work hard for what we want and continue to work hard to keep what we have. My story is no different. I'm certain that every life experience I've had up until this point has led me to where I am today, and I am a firm believer that everything I experience now is preparing me for something down the road.

OUTSTANDING ESTHETICS

The secret to becoming outstanding in esthetics has nothing to do with me or any other authors in this book. The opportunity to become outstanding lies within you. How bad do you want to be successful? Do you have what it takes to put in the extra work, leadership, and learning required? This is your chance to reevaluate how you're spending your time and what you're giving your energy to. We must make time for what we really want, and put hard work into getting where we want to be. The future is bright in skin care; the opportunities are boundless. It's up to you to get there.

In case you need a nudge: Your time is now. The time has come to set your career goals in motion and begin on the path to achieving your dreams.

It is my personal goal to give back in the same way others have helped build me up. If I can help you along your path to success, please reach out to me at lsnow@ascpskincare.com. Together, we can all achieve outstanding esthetics.

About Lauren Snow

Lauren Snow, executive director for Associated Skin Care Professionals, is a licensed esthetician with experience serving various fields in the skin care industry. Committed to helping nearly 17,000 members, Lauren evaluates the needs and missing skill sets of students and professionals to develop valuable membership benefit solutions. Combining her bachelor's degree in public relations and advertising with her vast knowledge of best skin care practices, Lauren spearheads ASCP's business development, including brand strategies, strategic partnerships, marketing campaigns, and membership collateral. Lauren enjoys speaking at national trade shows and writing for various industry trade publications. Her diverse role allows her to fulfill her goal of helping members become the best they can be, and she enjoys the satisfaction of watching them succeed.

Chapter 5

The Role of Microcurrent in Aesthetics

Authored by Tina Abnoosi

Throughout the past generations, our ancestors have always searched for ways to enhance their looks using many natural and artificial remedies. The science of anti-aging and a youthful look has always been on the forefront of human endeavors. The fundamental science-based research and understanding of the aging process is, however, relatively new.

Consumer demand has led to a growing need in this market and encouraged scientists and business developers to further explore this multibillion dollar market. Many products, procedures, and devices have recently flooded the market to meet the consumer demand. The investments in product and procedure development using modern medicine has surpassed beyond anyone's expectation. One of the recent areas of product development is in utilizing natural body's inflammation process by plumping the skin surface to combat the appearance of aging. In other words, these procedures are designed to take advantage of body's own healing function by purposefully creating a controlled level of trauma – such that it will ultimately stimulate the production of collagen, the natural filler that results in youthful skin. For example, procedures such as Microneedling, laser ablation and IPL PhotoFacial, all uses cellular disruption to activate the natural body's defense system to stimulate collagen production and create a more youthful look to the skin. Such approaches are based on a "quick fix" mentality, and the prolong use of it can lead to chronic inflammation. This constant inflammation is not only a precursor to disease, but may become the root of premature and long-term aging of the skin.

My search began after my aging mom undergone blepharoplasty and her beautiful eyes transformed. The change was so disproportionate that made the disappearance of the fine lines under the eyes and the lift of droopy eyelids insignificant. As an engineer and problem solver, I found myself with a new mission: I was determined to find a better cure, a natural treatment that could help us be younger looking – but not different. Finding the secret passage to the fountain of youth requires a great deal of understanding of how the body works, and how we can help remove micro-blockages and barriers so that the skin can reclaim its own health, and thus create and regenerate healthy cell turnover. So, my journey began! This journey led to an incredible amount of knowledge to share with the esthetic industry.

A method used in helping the body heal itself originates from ancient Greece, where they used electric eels to promote the healing of gout to reduce joint pain. Further research performed by physicians and scientists in the last 100 years revealed that small amounts of electric current is conducive in maintaining normal cell behavior by facilitating Iontophoresis – balancing Sodium,

Potassium, Chlorine ions in the cell – as well as aiding in the transportation of nutrients into, and toxins out of the cell.

As an electrical engineer who devoted her life designing magnetic components, realizing how our body works with electricity and the fact that each cell is safeguarded with a magnetic field was mind blowing. My discovery led me to my TMJ specialist who was using electrotherapy in treating my disjointed jaw. Receiving a small dose of electrical current, he explained, is a natural means of releasing muscle tension, rebuilding skin integrity and strengthening muscle fibers. Many devices manufactured to deliver small amount of current under 1000 micro amperes with different frequency selection settings allow one to manipulate different tissues. These devices are known as "Microcurrent" and are well sought-after by aesthetic, holistic and homeopathic professionals.

Based on my research, I decided to use this treatment on my severely handicapped daughter who suffered from severe complications of cerebral palsy throughout her entire life.

Wheelchair-bound, one struggle we tried to manage in the hopes of reducing her discomfort was relaxing her tight and spastic limbs. The procedure was lengthy, tedious and not very efficient, but I still found it to be far preferable to the alternative, more invasive, option.

The use of Microcurrent can be regarded as an auxiliary circuit to the natural brain-nervous system that is fundamentally based on an electrical stimulation network. This auxiliary "spare" system serves locally in order to replenish the lost messages that fail to be delivered due to natural aging. The effect of this modality is received by the body in the most natural and therapeutic form of treatment. The added electrotherapy helps alleviate pressure and frictional buildup, removes blockages by allowing the body to re-establish ionic exchange, and thus promotes homeostasis.

Studies have shown that Microcurrent increases fibroblast production – the base of collagen and elastin – which helps reduce fine lines and increase skin integrity. It simultaneously tones and rebuilds the muscles, regaining mass and facial firmness. Proper Microcurrent treatment can help release fascia, drain excess lymphatic fluid and increase in action potential. By increasing circulation, increased nutrient and oxygen flow helps increase the body's natural production of adenosine triphosphate ("ATP").

The reproduction of collagen using electrotherapy is very different than what is proposed through controlled trauma application, where the fibroblast production is created through natural and other processes which do not regenerate cell function but use what's in the body's emergency reservoir. Exhausting these reservoirs by losing them to antiaging procedure can leave the body without any help in the long run.

Here are a few noticeable outcomes of Microcurrent treatment:
- Helps brighten the skin and reduces the appearance of dark circles and other skin discoloration.
- Reduces puffiness and the bags under the eyes.
- Improves the appearance of fine lines, wrinkles and sagging skin.
- Helps skin appear firmer, lifted and toned.

- Its prolonged use will help reduce deep lines by increasing elastin and collagen production.

Microcurrent has found its niche in many other disciplines:

1. Cosmetic surgeons: Microcurrent accentuates the facial features and by adding it into invasive procedures such as Rhytidectomy and can help expedite healing and achieving better result.
   a. By providing a series of microcurrent treatment prior to surgery it may help remove blockages, strengthen the underlaying muscles which achieves better result.
   b. A series of treatments after the surgery may reduce inflammation and scar tissue buildup, therefore promoting faster healing.
2. Makeup Artists: The use of Microcurrent modality prior to makeup application enhances the facial features by:
   a. Lifting,
   b. Defining,
   c. Contouring, and significantly increasing makeover

effects.

3. Aesthetic professionals specialized in antiaging: This is one modality that they should not be without. Microcurrent offers sustainable results without damaging or invading the dermal layer and results in facial contouring. The continuous use of Microcurrent reduces the signs of stress and fatigue by increasing body's own healing ability resulting in total health. As a healthy body is a beautiful body! This holistic and noninvasive modality can elevate and set apart their services.

4. Acne Specialists: The use of Microcurrent can relieve the body from the toxins buried into the follicles resulting in a clear and even toned skin without the risk of scarring. Increased blood flow results in increased oxygen in the tissue, and improved lymphatic drainage aids in cellular waste removal. In many cases, the body repairs itself so the need for extractions is eliminated.

5. Aesthetic professionals specialized in treatment of darker skin types: As the risk of hyperpigmentation and keloid production is running high, care must be taken to employ a

modality that is safe and noninvasive. Microcurrent is one of the safest modalities to choose from where the risk of keloids formation and pigmentation is minimized and antiaging result is optimized.

The in-depth benefits of Microcurrent is yet to be fully understood by aesthetics and medical professionals. Many professionals are skeptical to offer this modality as various equipment have failed to meet the set expectations. In the recent years, there has been much improvement in technology and development of Microcurrent, reversing their view and beginning to realize the vast capabilities of this modality.

It is proven that those Microcurrent with intensity under 1000 UA are one of the safest modalities available to the aesthetic industry with effective results. However, one must be aware of the educational learning curve that it required to understand the correct techniques in order to deliver the expected result. Many treatments such as peels, dermaplaning or microdermabrasion require very little expertise in performing the stated treatment, whereas microcurrent treatment requires an in-depth understanding of facial muscles and mechanical structure. A professional who is interested to adopt this modality must be willing to set aside several hours a week to educate and train themselves. A well designed and produced device works in toning, building, and restructuring the facial features and by understating the underlaying issues can help prescribe a plan of treatment that delivers a superb facial lift. Proper use of this modality can promote facial symmetry, a commendable feature that can only be earned by facial surgery.

To make a body whole, the collaboration of modern and holistic medicine is inevitable and utilizing Microcurrent can be the gateway to healthy skin maintenance to not only stops the aging process but reversing the sign of time without the use of medicine and injectables.

About Tina Abnoosi

Tina Abnoosi is the founder, CEO and President of TAMA Research. She holds an Electrical Engineering degree and over 27 years of experience in design and manufacturing of electromagnetic components. With her creative mind, she has received many patents in different engineering disciplines.

Over the past 15 years, Tina's personal needs for Microcurrent therapy mandated her to learn this methodology. She then realized that the initial systems are far too complicated and cumbersome. She wanted to make a better mouse trap, a simpler device, and more integrative approach. The guiding principal was that in order to make this treatment available to many, it is essential to have a design that is simple to learn and intuitively easy to apply, yet effective, efficient, and ubiquitous. Together with Ali Shambayati, she founded TAMA Research.

Tina became a licensed aesthetician as she soon realized that in order for her to help her client's best, a thorough knowledge of what is taught in the field was necessary.

Tina leads all TAMA trainings and treatment protocols. Ms. Abnoosi believes that youthful look is a function of health and finds Microcurrent to be the most effective and noninvasive modality for staying healthy and young.

Contact Tina Today!

Email: tina@tamareserach.com

Chapter 6

Advancement in Esthetics Over the Last Three Decades

Authored by Michele Phelan

The esthetics industry is advancing at lightning speed and hardly resembles what it once was back in the mid-1980s when I began my journey into the world of skin care. In the 1980s many states like California did not even have the esthetician license. It was called a cosmetician license then and with the induction of the esthetician license some years later many estheticians, like me, were grandfathered into this new name licensing.

The term or title "esthetician" is new to the United States, in the same way, the practice of esthetics in the United States is new, compared to other countries. But the practice of skin care using facial massage, steam, herbs, essentials oils and other modalities has been utilized around the world for thousands of years to help treat the skin.

When I began my career most esthetic work performed by an esthetician was done in a spa or skin care salon and encompassed such treatments as basic cleansing or relaxing facials, facial and body waxing, makeup and other sorts of superficial treatments applied to the face. This is still the "bread and butter" of many salons and the heart of their core services. During the 1980s and 1990s, it was not common for an esthetician to work in a medical environment with a plastic surgeon, dermatologist or other medical doctors who specialize in the beauty and the health of the skin. Mainly because training was not available to estheticians like it is today and partially because most individuals who practiced skin care or cosmetic medicine did not see, at that time, the value and great benefits from having a physician/esthetician partnership.

With advancements in modern medicine, corrective skin care and greater education available as well as the emphasis placed on health and well-being, we are often living longer, healthier lives today than we were fifty years ago. With baby boomers moving into their golden years and generation X right behind them, we want to look as young as we feel. Not to mention the role that beauty manufacturers and the media play in rousing our psyches when it comes to touting youth and beauty. Modern technologies in skin care and aesthetic medicine lends itself to satisfying the beauty needs of this generation's women and men. Therefore, the need and demand for quality medical esthetic training for estheticians were subsequently realized.

High quality, advanced esthetic training is vital. Today it is not enough for an esthetician who wishes to work in the medical esthetic arena to only have a basic, superficial understanding of the skin. An esthetician must be a master of skin science, skin care products, ingredients and esthetic modalities used on the skin, to name a few things, and to understand how all of this works together on a profound level to benefit the client. To be able to satisfy the needs of clients (patients) who want to take advantage of these more profound services and to be able to effectively work with a physician synergistically, a higher level of esthetics education for estheticians is the gold standard.

There are many ways an esthetician and a physician can work together. I will go over some of those ways in this chapter. However, it is important to remember, each state has its own set of rules and regulations when it comes to what an esthetician can practice within the scope of their license. I literally get hundreds of inquiries each month from estheticians who have recently moved to California, the state in which my Para-medical esthetics training facility, Concepts Institute of Advanced Esthetics, is located. They ask why they can't use a lancet or fire a laser. Unknowingly, some estheticians may practice outside the scope of what their state board will allow until someone tells them it is not allowed. State laws are different from state to state and change from time to time. So it is important to find out what the laws in your state allow you to practice before working with clients. This will help to protect you and ensure your license is not in jeopardy.

Skin care should be every esthetician's core competency. However, an esthetician who works with a doctor needs to have knowledge that goes beyond just esthetics and skin care. The following are a few ways an esthetician and physician can unite for the benefit of the patient, the doctor, as well as the esthetician. For instance, you, the esthetician, may have your own skin care clinic or office and wish to have a referral system with a local physician. In this scenario, both of you can work in your respective offices in your own area of expertise and refer the mutual patient to one another when you find it to be advantageous to the patient. Having a rapport with a doctor in this way is great because when you have an issue or question that comes up that is out of your scope, you can contact the doctor for advice, direction or ideas and vice versa. You may also have the opportunity to work in a medical office either in your own treatment room or maybe in conjunction with the physician. In some states like California, a medical doctor can train and certify an individual as their medical assistant, and in many cases, they prefer to do this with licensed estheticians because of our great knowledge of the skin. If it is your goal to work as an assistant to the physician, it will behoove you to take a course or two in medical esthetics or find a physician's office willing to train you.

Medical Estheticians, so to speak, need to have knowledge of how a medical office works and how it is structured. Even though an esthetician may not be injecting neuromodulators, such as Botox, or soft tissue fillers, they must still have an understanding of how these chemicals work so they can educate the patients and understand the benefits of the treatments. Medical offices also have more stringent sterilization requirements, are required by law to document their patient's medical information in the patient's chart, and keep thorough medical records. Knowledge of basic medical terminology is essential so you can speak the same language as the rest of the staff and have the ability to read and write in a patient's chart accurately and effectively. If you are working with the doctor in their treatment room or the operating room, having knowledge of the surgical procedures the doctor performs and understanding wound care and healing is essential, as is the knowledge of certain medications and what they are used for.

There are many pre and post-surgical procedures that can be performed on the client's skin by an esthetician both before and after surgery to help speed up healing and improve the overall effect of the medical procedure. But for these treatments to be helpful and not potentially detrimental they need to be done correctly, and knowledgeably, and with great care. For instance, many of the physicians I work with request that the esthetician performs several hydrating and mildly exfoliating facials prior to facial plastic surgery, and a series of manual lymphatic drainage massage post-surgery to help decrease edema and bruising. Other doctors want the ultrasound modality to be used over surgical seams to help the healing process.

Many estheticians who work in a medical office specialize in acne. And once the doctor prescribes treatment, it is the esthetician's job to perform mild exfoliation, light skin extractions, and educate the client on home care. All of these procedures must be implemented by a well-trained esthetician and executed with expertise.

As Medical esthetics is becoming more common place. I often get questions from physicians who want to incorporate an esthetician into their practice but are not quite sure how to implement the process. Once I consult with them on the needs of their practice and lay out a game plan, their number one concern is that the esthetician they choose is a professional. And of course, the professional needs to be an expert in skin care, able to educate patients and make them feel comfortable, and be able to self-manage. The doctors are happy to be there to answer questions, but because of their busy, demanding schedules, they don't want nor have the time to micro-manage.

Having had several skin care companies and the great opportunity to train and work with many phenomenal, nurturing and truly first rate estheticians over the last thirty years, I can see that the future of esthetics looks bright and beautiful. With so many talented individuals joining the industry every year, ours is an industry that is looked up to and admired. Whether you are a seasoned esthetician or a newbie, whether you are an esthetician who wants to perform relaxing, luxurious skin care or more corrective, clinical treatments, staying informed and well educated, will keep you relevant and on top of your game. And most importantly, help you retain an appreciative, loyal clientele for many years.

About Michele Phelan

Michele Phelan has been a licensed esthetician for over 30 years and a CIDESCO diplomat for over 15. She has had several skin care clinics and a full service spa located in San Francisco, Ca. Michele still maintains a semi-full time skin care practice. She has taught esthetics at every level including: state board, CIDESCO, and other medical and clinical curriculum. She has served as a CIDESCO examiner and helped to develop the CIDESCO curriculum at Ms. Marty's beauty college, the first college in California to have this acclaimed international program. Michele is a sought after guest speaker at esthetics symposiums around the nation. She is a registered aromatherapist and is the formulator and owner of Serum Essentials a professional aromatherapy skin and body care line.

Being a visionary, Michele realized in the 1980s that the esthetics industry was in great need of high quality, expertly trained estheticians to be able to satisfy the more complex beauty needs of those who seek esthetics services. In 2008 after being asked for decades by estheticians and physicians alike to develop a program that helped to bridge the two, she developed and founded Concepts Institute of Advanced Esthetics. Here she writes and teaches the core curriculum for the Clinical Esthetics course and in conjunction with Dr. Bradley Greene, MD, MBA FACS, writes and teaches part of the Para-medical esthetics course. In 2017 the duo launched their on-line para-medical esthetics course so that it would be available to estheticians around the nation and globally.

Michele states that one of her greatest professional achievements was not just to be able to share her wealth of knowledge with other estheticians but to foster and mentor them in their own professional growth to help them become esthetic leaders themselves.

Michele has authored many articles in such publications as Dermascope, Skin Inc. Skin Deep, Les Nouvelle on topics such as medical esthetics, aromatherapy, modalities, skin care ingredients and business to name a few. She has authored many articles in local news paper and has been interviewed by CBS on the benefit of lash extensions.

Contact Michele Today!

Concepts Institute of Advanced Esthetics

Address: 341 West Lake Center (medical/dental Bldg.) #245 Daly City (Bay Area), CA 94015

Email: conceptsmmp@gmail.com

Website: http://www.conceptsinstitute.com

Chapter 7

Life Changing Esthetics

Authored by Becky Kuehn

Life changing Esthetics! Wow, that's a powerful statement, what do I mean by that? I believe as Estheticians we have the power to change lives. How? By listening first, then using our touch, talents, and tools we can transform our clients, so they leave feeling as beautiful on the outside as they are on the inside. And, science (reference 1 below) shows that we also benefit and are fundamentally changed when we help others. That's what I call life changing!

Have you ever had a client touch you so deeply you were profoundly changed? First I want to share with you a little bit of my story, and then I will introduce you to the beautiful soul that put me on a new path, forever changing me and the course of my life.

Why oncology? My personal experience with cancer started with a diagnosis at the age of 18. I had graduated high school just a year before, was in "Beauty School," my whole life ahead of me, (or so I thought). Engaged to my high school sweetheart, our upcoming wedding had us busy and excited, planning our future. I was exhausted, got a cold sore and had a period that did not stop. And although I knew this wasn't right, my doctor assured me it was most likely related to stress and nothing to worry about. We made it through the wedding and headed off for our honeymoon. But one day into it, I started to hemorrhage and ended up in the emergency room. Not how you envision your honeymoon, right?

They "fixed" me up and we headed home. Two weeks later, I received a phone call from my doctor. I'm sure there is no great way to say this but, he very clinically informed me "you have cancer, blah, blah, blah." At that moment, my world changed. Once he said the "C" word, I didn't hear anything else. I could see the future I had planned disappearing. I went through a full range of emotions and thoughts one has when faced with life-threatening news: fear, denial, anger and a sense of loss.

It was a year of life lessons in faith, strength, and how a cancer diagnosis affects not just the person going through it, but their entire tribe. I had countless doctor visits, needles, drugs, side effects, and revelations. I hope you never have to experience it, but for those who have, you know what I'm talking about. The good news is that for many people, a cancer diagnosis changes them for the better. They begin to see life differently; they appreciate the small things and are happy to be alive. Once, I was concerned with wrinkles and pimples, but now they seemed so insignificant as I was dealing with collapsed veins, mucositis (pain and inflammation of the mucous membrane), high fevers, nausea, malaise, hair thinning and the possibility of no children and not getting through this chapter of my life. But, deep inside, I knew that I *would* get through this, and I needed to find a way to give back and help others on this journey.

But as life does, it goes on, and I got on with my life. With my cancer, I wasn't supposed to be able to have children, but God had another plan for me and blessed me with three. When they were teenagers (there's another life lesson!), we were out shopping together one day when I noticed the way the store clerk looked at my son with his saggy pants and blue hair. As his mom, I knew his heart, and I knew he was a good kid. It broke my heart to see how quickly we tend to look at the outside of a person and pass judgment. I asked God to let me see people as he sees them, to allow me to see their hearts and their souls. The ability to look *in* and not *at* someone has changed me and prepared me for what was to come. (Just a side note, that blue-haired teenager is an artist who manages a team at Microsoft).

"Give before you get" was something I always believed in so never forgetting my past, I started volunteering with the American Cancer Society's Look Good Feel Better program. I gained experience and developed a love for working with oncology clients. As I listened to their challenges and struggles, I realized that sadly, in 30 years, not much had changed. As I reflected on my past, my goal and challenge became clear.

I began to research everything I could on cancer, looking for ways I could offer help, hope, and encouragement. I developed an idea for an ongoing, customized program that would meet the unique needs of each client. I set up a meeting with the Women's Breast Center Manager, pitched my vision to her, and she responded: "Hmmm…well…interesting. I will talk with the Medical Director and get back to you." As I walked to the car, I was already thinking about my follow up and what I would do or present next. But, as I started my car, the phone rang; it was her, and she said YES!!!!!

We set up a small treatment room in the center, and I introduced myself to all the staff in the doctor's offices, cancer center, and hospital so they would know who I was and how I could help. Then something incredible happened. I got a call from the local newspaper. They were contacting me about advertising, but, I mistakenly assumed they wanted to interview me, so I prepped for my time in the "spotlight." I started the meeting by talking about my passion, what I do, why I do it, where I was located, etc. and the salesperson just looked at me and cried. She shared her story of cancer in her family and how she loved what I was doing and would pass it on to the editor. The next thing I knew, I was a feature article. (Big success tip here!)

Now, remember the client I mentioned at the beginning that changed me? Let me introduce you to Jatin, a stage four stomach cancer patient at the end of his life. No treatments had worked for him, and in fact, his cancer had now metastasized (moved to other parts of his body). He shared his story with me, and my heart broke for him and his family. I asked him if he was experiencing any skin issues or if there was something I could help with. He put both arms out and said his skin was very dry. So, I applied body lotion to his hands and arms as we continued to talk. At the end of our time together, I told him how nice it was to meet him and invited him to come back to see me. I held my hand out to shake his hand, but instead, he took my hand, kissed it and held it to his face. He softly said, "Thank you, you have no idea how I have thirsted for touch like that." With a quivering lip, all I could say was "you're welcome."

I packed my things, headed to the car and as soon as I sat down, I broke into tears. Although I had many thoughts in my head, I realized something amazing had just happened! How were two strangers able to connect and change each other's lives in such a short span of time? The answer is "touch!" Touch connects us as human beings. Touch is critical. We have, as a society and even in Esthetics, walked away from simple touch and its healing powers. We now have available to us all kinds of results driven, effective equipment, which is wonderful, but they have taken the place of us touching our clients. We **CAN'T** forget to touch; we need it, our clients need it. I even have some clients who say it is **THE** very reason they come in. **NEVER** underestimate the power of touch.

That encounter was my **WOW** moment and confirmed that I was made to work with oncology clients. It has become my life's work and mission to share with others so that together we can increase the reach of healing hands. It's wonderful to see the changes, not only in me but also in my clients, and the many thanks I receive from our grads who have taken the Life Changing Esthetics, Oncology-Trained course. The power is yours – use it!

Success tips for changing lives:

- Find out what you were made to do and then passionately do it.
- Learn all you can and never stop learning.
- Find a way to serve others.
- Create unique, customized treatments, give your clients something to talk about and a reason to come back to you.
- Last, but most important: Touch your clients, change some lives!

Becky has a new book launching in the Fall of 2017 called "Beautiful Souls…Help, Hope and Encouragement for the cancer journey." A resource guide for you, your clients, family and loved ones as they journey through cancer.

References:

1. http://mentalfloss.com/article/71964/7-scientific-benefits-helping-others, (Helps you live longer, Altruism is contagious, makes us happy, helps relieve chronic pain, lowers blood pressure, helps teens behave, gives us a sense of purpose and satisfaction)

2. http://www.huffingtonpost.com/2016/12/12/international-day-of-happiness-helping-_n_6905446.html (Makes you feel great, boosts self-esteem, strengthens friendships, raises optimism, gives you a sense of belonging, helps you feel thankful and feel your own inner peace and a sense of renewal).

3. http://www.webmd.com/balance/features/science-good-deeds#1 (The science of good deeds: We each have the innate need to do good, kindness is linked to good health, happiness in the brain, affects oxytocin/the healing hormone)

About Becky Kuehn

Founder of Oncology Spa Solutions®
Licensed Master Esthetician, Cosmetologist, Hope Coach, Educator

Becky is the passionate founder of Oncology Spa Solutions®. Her mission along with her team of angel trainers is to share with others how to care for clients when they have cancer, connect with Dr's and make a difference in their communities. Join her in changing lives!

Contact Becky Today!

Website: http://www.oncologyspasolutions.com
Email: Becky@oncologyspasolutions.com

Chapter 8

How To Build A Successful Skin Care Business The S.M.A.R.T. Way

Authored by Beverlee Garb, M.P.A.

You went to school to become an esthetician. Now, you want to make a living with this skill. It is harder than you thought, right? Most of us got our esthetics license because we love helping others – we love healing through touch and offering solutions to skin care issues. And yet, no matter how good we are at our trade, we find ourselves faced with the daunting task of creating a steady stream of loyal clients.

You are not alone. In my twenty years in the beauty industry, as an esthetician, skin care trainer, spa owner, and spa director, I have seen many estheticians struggle to make a steady income while working in their craft. Building a career is not something we learn in school. It is an art developed by making mistakes and then picking ourselves up to try again, hopefully, learning new skills along the way.

In this chapter, I am happy to share with you the lessons I have learned, all of which culminated in a surprisingly simple approach to building a successful skin care business: The S.M.A.R.T. Approach, a path to succeed at work through Strategy, Milestones, Alignment, Results and Trust (S.M.A.R.T.).

Strategy: S.M.A.R.T. skin care technicians know their destination. They point their arrow in the direction that makes the most sense for their values and goals. As a business consultant, I have spoken to many estheticians who are so busy with day-to-day operations they have lost their vision.

Where do you want to be in five years? Do you want to have your own room and set your own schedule? Do you want to work for a large spa and have all the resources they bring? Would you like to own your own business and have a team of technicians working for you?

S.M.A.R.T. Tip: Write out your FIVE YEAR GOAL. Caution: do not write "should" goals – where you think you "should" be in five years. Do some soul-searching and plan from your heart. What do you truly want and need to be happy? If keeping it small and simple fits your lifestyle better than managing other people and dealing with the complexities of a larger organization, then stay true to your values.

Milestones: S.M.A.R.T. estheticians set attainable, measurable steps to achieve their business vision. Without milestones, you may end up somewhere you never intended.

I was on a business cruise last year. We traveled to Spain and Italy facilitating a leadership development workshop – I know, my job is awful! The third day was a free day. We could get off the boat and go to a few pre-selected destinations. I chose Cinque Terra – five beautiful fishing villages set amid the most dramatic coastal scenery. I traveled to this quaint destination in my teens and knew I couldn't miss it. My roommate decided to come along. We put on our sneakers and sunscreen and prepared for our day out.

Mel (my roommate) and I had so much in common that there was never a dull moment. We chatted about work, family and our lives back home. As we were gabbing, we noticed a stream of joggers kept whizzing by – running passed us, and then passed again and then again. Something was not right. All of a sudden, Mel looks at me, and in her Australian accent she says, "Bloody-hell, we are on the jogging track!" We had missed the doorway to the tour bus and had been circling the boat. That was it. We missed our destination and spent the day trapped on the boat instead.

Business is not unlike this experience. If you get too distracted by the noise of seeing clients and forget to stay on track, you will end up somewhere other than your intended destination. Milestones help you take time out from the busyness and re-evaluate the direction you are heading.

S.M.A.R.T. Tip: Set daily, weekly, and monthly milestones. How many clients do you need to see in a day to earn your desired income? How many hours do you want to work during the week? How many hours do you want to leave free for hobbies, family or exercise? Where would you like to be in five years? If you are not where you want to be at your milestone evaluations, some elements of your business may need shifting.

Alignment: S.M.A.R.T. technicians are purpose-driven and understand thatwhat they want to achieve for themselves and their business will benefit humanity in a deep and meaningful way. They base their decisions on the 'Alignment Factor' – aligning with a cause they care about so deeply it influences all of their decisions.

S.M.A.R.T. Tip: Weave purpose into your business. Ask questions such as, "when you were younger, did you feel you were born to make a difference? In what way? Have you ever dreamed that your work would make the world a better place? How? What do your friends rely on you for – what gifts do you bring to your relationships?" As you dig deeper into this inquiry, you will notice you have always been living true to your purpose. You cannot help it – it is your essence that shines out into the world and draws others towards you.

Results: The days of being successful by giving a great massage and focusing on pampering are over. Clients are savvy and demand a results-oriented approach to skin care. A lot has changed over the years, and when it comes to the skincare industry, things tend to change rapidly. What this means for estheticians is we need to stay current with trends, ingredients and innovative technology to keep clients coming back.

According to dermatologists, there is an unprecedented demand for the "buzz" ingredients such as hyaluronic acid, retinol, peptides and other new, innovative anti-aging techniques, such as Glutathione and the Noble Prize winning Epidermal Growth Factor (EGF). There is also an increased interest in deeper peels and aggressive treatments.

While many of these ingredients and treatments have previously been available only to the medical community, they are now accessible by estheticians. If you are looking for effective products containing these "corrective ingredients," Biodroga MD is my go-to. This line offers medical skin care without a prescription – and avoids ingredients which may irritate the skin, such as parabens, mineral oil, emulsifiers, and PEG. For more information, visit biokosmetikoftexas.com or call 1-800-729.1242.

If you are looking for a natural alternative to chemical peels, one that is safe to be administered by estheticians without the supervision of a doctor, THE GREEN PEEL by Dr. Schrammek is my favorite. This peel is a mixture of eight selected herbs, containing enzymes, minerals, and vitamins, which are massaged into the skin. Without the use of chemical or surgical procedures, this peel stimulates collagen production, reduces signs of aging and reduces chronic skin conditions such as acne, scars, and hyperpigmentation. For more information, visit biokosmetikoftexas.com or call 1-800-729.1242.

S.M.A.R.T. Tip: When it comes to corrective skin care, do your homework. Make sure the products and technology you pick create visible results and align with your overall strategy and values. If you are a holistic technician, then choose protocols that align with this choice. If you are attracted to medical esthetics, then choose products and equipment that allow you to offer more aggressive treatments.

Trust: Trust is the benchmark of an effective skin care business. Building a community based on trust and communication will create long-term, sustainable clients. In addition to treating clients well when they are in your treatment room, build an email list and stay in touch with them. Newsletters, emails, webinars with ongoing education and communication help your clients feel they are part of something larger than skin care.

S.M.A.R.T. Tip: Build your email list. This can be done through opt-in forms on your website, collecting emails when clients visit your business, joint ventures with other businesses that have your target clients, etc. Then, stay in touch. Wish them happy birthday and anniversary, thank them for their first visit, send educational information on related topics such as health and wellness and ask them for their feedback. Like any relationship, showing you care will go a long way.

In conclusion, I invite you to take an honest look at what is working in your career as an esthetician and what needs some attention. Do not beat yourself up; there are likely some areas in which you excel and others in which you could improve. It all begins with being honest and having a willingness to develop yourself as an esthetician, a business person, and a leader.

About Beverlee Garb, M.P.A.

Beverlee Garb, M.P.A. specializes in digital marketing for skin care professionals. Her passion is designing & optimizing web/e-commerce sites and driving more traffic to your business. She has been in the skin care industry for 20+ years – as an esthetician, spa owner, spa director and spa consultant – and understands how to navigate the digital landscape to help you thrive in the age of the internet.

For a Free Consult, Contact Beverlee Today!

Email: |info@beverleegarb.com

Phone: 760-500-6332

Chapter 9

The Discovery of the Sea's Most Powerful Antioxidant and the Launch of RéjuvaSea

Authored by Frederic Fouassier

It all started in March 2009, on a cool Tuesday morning in Seville, Spain. It was 4:30 AM when my alarm clock went off. I was jet lagged…

You see, it took me three stops and over 25 hours to get here from California. I arrived in Seville the night before, met an old friend and sat outside an outdoor café at one of Seville's magical squares. We enjoyed tapas and drank way too much Rioja.

I finally turned off the alarm clock, loaded myself up with caffeine, went downstairs and waited for my car.

March is the best time of the year to visit Seville when thousands of orange trees offer a true spectacle and fill the air with the scent of blossoms. However, I didn't come here to visit the sensual Andalusian capital, but I came to visit a Natural Preserve called Veta La Palma, experience a natural phenomenon and connect it with anti-aging and skincare.

As we zipped through the old town and headed south for a 50-minute drive, I couldn't help feeling the excitement building in my stomach. In an article written about me a couple of years ago, I was described as a serial entrepreneur, outside-the-box thinker and diverse early stage operator. From Wall Street to Software to Skincare, my core strength is the ability to embrace new concepts in a very short time and architect scalable, high-valued solutions that disrupt markets. What I didn't know then was that the next six hours were going to change my life and, within months, I was going to become the CEO of a skincare company. But, I am getting ahead of myself.

My destination, Veta La Palma is one of the largest, most important sustainable marine sanctuaries in the world. Over 250 different species of birds feed daily in its abundant waters. Scientists have observed that some species, like the flamingo, fly 150 miles every day to feed on the marine life in the preserve. That is what I came here to experience, thousands of flamingos making the daily trip.

The million-dollar question: What would compel this daily journey to Veta la Palma? There had to be something special in the water. We brought in a number of scientists, started to study the preserve and we discovered the flamingo knew something we didn't. This preserve was rich with marine phytoplankton, an extraordinary antioxidant, and source of fatty acids, vitamins, minerals and amino acids.

There have been over 3,500 strains of marine phytoplankton discovered in different parts of the world. After clinical studies, we realized that our scientists identified the most potent strain of marine phytoplankton*, found only in the waters of this private sanctuary, Veta la Palma in Southern Spain.

Why is Marine Phytoplankton so important?

Oceans cover more than 70 percent of the earth's surface, and these oceans are the habitat of up to 90 percent of the planet's organisms. Oceans provide many unique environments and rich resources, and there is an endless number of marine organisms, but only one group, marine phytoplankton, is the key to all other's existence. The origin of marine phytoplankton (microalgae) dates back 2.5 billion years. These organisms were responsible for the production of oxygen that turned the atmosphere of our planet into a "breathable" environment allowing the development of other life forms. Today, NASA says marine phytoplankton produce 50 percent of the oxygen we breathe. Microalgae have a tremendous impact on the sustainability of the marine ecosystem, being the primary producer and, therefore, a food source for other marine organisms.

Does Marine Phytoplankton protect against free radicals?

The ability of marine phytoplankton to fight against oxidative stress is one of the main factors that influence its survival in the marine environment. These organisms have been adapted to extremely harsh and competitive environments by producing a number of compounds and secondary metabolites for survival, and are thus able to live in a wide range of ecological niches. For instance, microalgae have developed survival strategies based on the synthesis of highly protective antioxidant compounds. The antioxidative defense system includes enzymatic and non-enzymatic components. Among the enzymatic system, superoxide dismutase (SOD) is the first and most important of the antioxidant metalloenzymes. Naturally occurring in every aerobic organism, SOD protects virtually every cell from harmful free radicals toxicity and also acts as a powerful anti-inflammatory.

How about Marine Actives and absorption?

We are asked this question all the time. The depths of the ocean acts as a simple filtration system against the UV rays so the nutrients in seawater and species of microalgae could form and flourish.

There are also many similarities between a marine environment and the composition of our bodies.

Did you know that seawater and blood plasma have a nearly identical chemical composition in terms of mineral and trace element levels?

Seawater is so close to the body's internal environment that if white blood cells are removed from the body and placed in a sterile diluted seawater solution, they are able to maintain normal cell function. This is the only solvent that will allow for continued cellular activity. In other words, marine actives get absorbed at the cellular level at a higher level than nature based botanicals and are clinically proven to increase skin hydration, improve skin clarity and repair skin elasticity.

After we had received the results of the clinicals, we knew that we had most of the pieces of the puzzle in place to introduce a different type of professional skincare line. We had exclusive access to our preserve and our proprietary active ingredient, the Sea's Most

Powerful Antioxidant*. Furthermore, since we had our own active ingredient, we realized that we had tremendous flexibility in the concentration of the key active in the formulation. In the RéjuvaSea Skincare Labs, we believe in the beauty of science and the power of nature, and this led to the creation of a professional, marine-based skincare line with a high concentration of the key active to ensure our customers experience the benefits we promise. There was only one piece of the puzzle missing. As RéjuvaSea grew, were we going to deplete Veta La Palma from the Marine Phytoplankton?

Our commitment

To avoid depleting the natural resources of Veta la Palma, we replicated this nutrient-rich ecosystem at the RéjuvaSea® research and development facility in Cadiz, Spain, and designed an innovative method for sustainable harvesting of RéjuvaPlankton® in an eco-friendly facility. The commitment was the preservation of Veta la Palma. As one of the world's last unspoiled sanctuaries, we wanted to make sure we were not going to deplete our preserve of this incredible resource. This led to the design of sustainable harvesting and extraction methods that protect the natural resources of this special ecosystem. Our goal was for our sanctuary to remain unspoiled and continue to inspire us with its natural beauty.

This entire process took us from 2009 to 2014...five years to perfect. So what's happened since then?

After two years of marketing to the professional Skincare Industry, in early 2017, we received the prestigious Esthetician Choice Award for our Night Cream in the Night Moisturizer category. We also finished second in the Exfoliating Cleanser and Oil Free Moisturizer category.

As the CEO, I have learned so much about this industry and what it takes to be successful. I am thankful beyond words to my team, and I appreciate their trust in my abilities to lead. Catherine Lima, you are an angel, thank you for everything you do, both at home and for the business. I will also always be grateful to my partners in Spain and Canada for their support and commitment to our success. Like many other businesses, we needed a major differentiation factor, story, positioning and ingredient. More importantly, we needed to commit to train our customers and then train them again and again.

While this is a very competitive industry it is also an industry based on relationships and trust. In order to achieve success, we needed to be patient and let other people share their results and success stories about RéjuvaSea. We also needed to find the right marketing partners and spend most of our time traveling to trade shows and workshops around the country so we could continue to build those relationships and trust. At times it wasn't easy, but every step was worth it.

I'd like to send a major shout-out to Shelley Hancock with Shelley Hancock Consulting, she has a total passion for Estheticians and helping them reach their goals. I would also like to thank Jennifer Rosenblum with The Skin Games. We are now one of the major sponsors of The Skin Games, and we love how progressive this community is. Jennifer has created the most unique and exciting skincare event in the world, and I love being a part of that.

Our story can be your story. It is about getting started, keep going forward and knowing what you can bring to the industry. For us, we feel that we have just gotten started, and we now have so much more to bring to this industry. We can't wait to see what happens and who we'll meet next.

*Claim based on Clinical Studies conducted by the Agricultural University of Athens (AUA), Greece.

About Frederic Fouassier

Frederic Fouassier is the Co-Founder, CEO and Managing Member of Global Marine Phytoplankton Company, LLC. http://www.rejuvasea.com. Fred is a serial entrepreneur, outside-the-box thinker and diverse early stage operator. From Wall Street to Software to Skincare, his core strength is the ability to embrace new concepts in a very short time and architect scalable, high-valued solutions that disrupt markets. Fred was born and educated in France and moved to the US in 1994. He now leaves in Reno, Nevada and with his family enjoys everything that Lake Tahoe has to offer.

Chapter 10

The Psychology of Getting Paid Your Worth

Authored by Grace Mosgeller

You love transforming skin. You love seeing and feeling the delight, joy, and satisfaction of your customers. You love giving treatments and the business you created. It's fun and rewarding, but for some people, even though you've implemented the best marketing/business strategies, it's been hard to create an income that fuels your life. You don't want to give up on your dream, but you do need to make a sustainable income. What to do?

It is true that following any proven business and marketing systems will help most estheticians succeed. But, I have found that many self-employed people can unknowingly hold themselves back by missing out on the most important, foundational key to profits and success that most of us are unaware we need: a mindset of success.

Failure or success in the skin care business, or any business, is the result of cumulative decisions and actions. While some people seem lucky in business, it really isn't luck, an accident or fate that creates success. It is your mindset. What you believe about yourself, money, and success, drive your decisions and actions and lead to the profitable results you are after.

Here are four mindset strategies successful people use. I believe these strategies can help make the difference between success and failure.

#1 Take Responsibility for Everything that Happens to You.

In the world of personal development and success, taking 100 percent responsibility for what happens in your life is fundamental if you want to thrive and become successful.

When you don't take responsibility, you give up your power and become a victim. You lose control of what you could do to remedy the situation because your energy is focused on blaming and complaining.

Most of us think we are taking responsibility for our lives already, but sometimes, places, where we are not taking responsibility, can show up in ways that we aren't fully aware of. The easiest way to identify where you might not be taking responsibility is to notice when you complain so you can do something about it.

Become super aware, super mindful, and write down complaints as you notice them. The act of observation helps you to become complaint free. When they are written down, you can make a plan to correct the source of irritation. And your power is regained.

Maybe customers are late or don't show, or don't purchase retail or don't rebook, or a snow day tanks your schedule, or you don't have that super-duper website or cool esthetic equipment, or something costs too much, or the economy sucks, or a family member did or didn't do something annoying . . .

I am not suggesting that you ignore annoying situations, rather that you do something about it. Solve the problem. Put a system in place or set a boundary around your complaint, and keep your personal power focused on success.

When you commit to becoming complaint free, you have more energy and power to focus on what really matters in your business.

#2 Adopt an Entrepreneurial Mindset

The scariest part about working for yourself is that unlike being an employee, you must put yourself out there and represent you.

Employees have a buffer between themselves and who they serve. They just do their job. Their ego is not on the line because they are being paid to support someone else's business vision.

As an entrepreneur, your business is a reflection of you. What you believe in, what you care about and value. You are the one who creates your business vision as you want it to look and how it serves others. Which feels very exciting and freeing, right? It also can feel very scary. Because if someone doesn't like you, or something about your business, that can feel like a personal rejection. Not only does rejection feel bad, but most of us will do anything to avoid feeling it, which leads to self-sabotaging behaviors that thwart our progress.

Maybe it feels uncomfortable charging what seems a lot, or it's too stressful to "put yourself out there" marketing yourself at networking events, making videos, aligning strategically with other businesses, or meeting potential customers while you are out and about.

An employee mindset believes that personal time is traded for money and you do everything yourself. An entrepreneur mindset leverages systems, and support staff to manifest money on demand. The quicker you find people and systems to support you, the quicker you'll create a business that makes money to fuel you and your life. Yes, it is really easy to say, "I don't have the money or the resources to bring other people on." When you embrace that you can't do it all, you'll become very resourceful and creative so you can attract the right people to help you.

There are inexpensive marketing assistants online in the Philippines. (http://www.onlinejobs.ph). And, you can trade with coaches, mentors, and accountants. It is possible to find affordable support; you just have to look for and believe it's there for you.

Remember, you can never get your time back, once it's gone, it's gone. You can always get more money, but you can never get back time.

#3 Money, Success and Self-Love Blocks

These are the blind spots in our life. They are unconscious beliefs we don't even think about but run our everyday decision making and action taking. When these hidden beliefs are in conflict with and contradict the desires we have they totally get in the way of our success.

We pick up these beliefs when we are very young and become our reality. There are superficial beliefs such as money does not grow on trees, or money is not spiritual, or too much success and power make you corrupt, or too much success means you'll lose friends. And there are deeper core beliefs about your value and worth in the world that also get in the way of success.

Bruce Lipton, Ph.D., author of the Biology of Belief, says 90 percent of what we believe about ourselves is unconscious and rooted in the wisdom of a child. When it comes to making important decisions about your business, do you really want to make them from the perspective of an eight-year-old?

So how do you know if you have these blocks to money and success? Self-sabotaging blocks leave clues to let us know they need to be taken care of. They can show up as:

- Lots of effort and hustle, with little to no reward
- Avoidance, or procrastination to do the exact things that bring your business
- Waiting for perfection or not finishing a project, before starting a new one
- Impenetrable income ceilings, debt that never goes away or disappearing savings
- Never asking for help, or, never getting support when you ask for it
- Stress eating, stress shopping…anything to distract from the task at hand

Working with a coach trained in Emotional Freedom Techniques (EFT) or "tapping" can gently clear the origins of these blind spots permanently.

#4 Believe In Magic

Believe in the magic of miracles that can show up in life.

I believe that we are all meant to thrive and have extraordinary lives, but that's not just given to us, we must choose it. And we have to be willing to do whatever it takes every single day to create success for ourselves. If you have a desire for something, a yearning, an outcome that you are dying for, then it is, in fact, inevitable. It's an absolute possibility if you are willing to do what it takes.

My heart breaks when I see people with drive and desire take action and then at one point just give up. They decide "I can't ever have that" or "that is just not me," or "It's not meant for me." I personally don't believe that way. I feel if the desire is there, how in the heck did it get there? Where did it come from? If it's within you, then you get to create it. Any idea in your head can become a reality.

Dreams become reality when you have faith, believe in yourself, and your business, as you take action with confidence and conviction and have lots of gratitude for where you are right now.

Having a skin care business that fuels your life doing what you love is your Divine right. If you find yourself struggling, even after implementing the best-proven strategies, your mindset is in your way. Become aware of your mindset. Take responsibility for money and success blocks. Do the work to shift, clear and heal them, and get paid your worth running the business of your dreams.

About Grace Mosgeller

Grace Mosgeller is a retired solo esthetician who after clearing her own blocks to love, money and success, now guides women entrepreneurs to do the same. She's put together a FREE, three-part video resource called: "Tap Away Money Blocks" tailored just for estheticians. Grab it here

https://gracemosgeller.com/moneyblocksestys/

Contact Grace today!

Website: https://gracemosgeller.com

Chapter 11

Bringing Nutrition to Skincare Professionals

The Healing Power of Nutrition – My Personal Experience

Authored by Ginger Hodulik Downey

I am passionate about the power of nutrition and positive lifestyle habits to transform lives! My love of the nutrition field was inspired by personal experiences: First, my mother who battled obesity and its associated disease states her entire life, and also my own personal experience with the healing power of nutrition that began 18 years ago as I struggled with autoimmune disease. I watched my Mom suffer for years with diseases and chronic pain caused by her weight. All of her health conditions were a result of her poor food choices and overeating, yet she could not seem to change. My entire life I worried about her and longed to figure out a way to help my Mom, and people like her free themselves from the grip of food addiction. In my case, it was not about weight; it was about health. My health problems began after the birth of my second son. I experienced an "autoimmune storm" no doctor could seem to help me calm. I was overcome by skin rashes, joint pain, exhaustion and a sluggish metabolism. I was offered numerous prescriptions for antidepressants (which I tossed in the trash), but no one ever took the time to get to the heart of what was stimulating my immune system into overdrive. I distinctly remember a doctor telling me that I looked too good to be sick, and that I should try taking naps when my babies napped. In my frustration I began researching – and ultimately used nutrition and lifestyle changes – not pharmaceutical drugs – to heal my body. It was empowering!

Education, the Path Forward in my Career

The success I experienced in my life using food as a healing tool sealed the deal for me and made me a true believer in the power of nutrition. I vowed to make it my life goal to help others like my Mom and me, so I went back to school nights and weekends while working part-time and raising my children. It took some time, but eventually I earned a BS in Foods & Nutrition, an MS in Nutrition, and a CNS designation, which required 1,000 hours of supervised clinical practice. It was critically important to me to have a solid science background in place before getting to work in the field. There is so much false and conflicting information out there on nutrition, and I wanted to ensure I could sort out fact from fiction to make meaningful recommendations. After completing my education, I began a career in workplace wellness. In that role, I was able to touch thousands of people with our wellness coaching program. It made my heart full to see people transform themselves through wellness. From weight loss to sports nutrition, we helped people set goals and use nutrition and lifestyle changes to reach them. I learned that sometimes it is not about what I know about the science of nutrition, but rather it's about helping people progress through the stages of change to implement new habits. This was a huge "ah ha" moment for me. When the corporation I was working for decided to sell our business unit, a co-worker and I wondered if we could somehow bring our wellness expertise to an industry that was not really focused on wellness, yet should be, so we began shopping for a company.

Transition to the Skincare Field

In July of 2011, Mark Pinsley and I bought DermaMed Solutions, a company that manufactures equipment and a skincare line for aesthetic professionals. When I heard about the opportunity, I lit up! As a Clinical Nutritionist I know that our skin health is a reflection of our gut health, and by healing our digestive systems, we can calm inflammatory skin conditions and slow cell aging. At that time wellness was just beginning to enter the spa space. Everyone knew it belonged there, but no one could figure out how to incorporate wellness into this setting. Our vision for DermaMed Solutions was to be the whole-istic provider of skincare solutions, providing products and services that address all aspects of skincare, considering the whole person and all the inputs that contribute to skin health. Our logo represents the three components – mechanical treatments, topical treatments and wellness inputs. I am thrilled to be in this unique position as the only skincare company owned by a nutrition professional, putting together all of the pieces for healthy, brilliant skin.

My first order of business with DermaMed was ensuring the skincare products we sold were clean. What I mean by clean is free of endocrine system disrupting chemicals and ingredients that could cause harm. Examples include: parabens, sulfates, phthalates, artificial colors, and fragrances. We tapped natural botanical extracts as the source of our active ingredients and nutrients because our skin thrives on plant-based nutrition, just like our bodies. Every single day our skin needs topical vitamins, like A and C, along with antioxidants like those found in green tea and vitamin E to defend against free radical damage. The result is our dmSkincare™ line, which creates well-nourished skin from the outside-in.

My next project was figuring out how to get the word out to an audience that, in the past was sorely under informed about nutrition – doctors and aestheticians. Seems crazy, doesn't it? These professionals are in a perfect position to help people with wellness tools to support the skin, yet they receive little to no formal training on the subject. We began holding educational seminars and continuing education talks where I lectured on the intricacies of nutrition and lifestyle choices for skin health. I also offered private training and began writing for skin industry trade journals and blogs. The response has been amazing! After my talks people line up with questions about how they can help their clients, while staying within their scope of practice. Skincare professionals are thirsty for this type of information. I created handouts and tools for our customers to share with their clients so they have credible, science-based handouts and resources to use in practice. This type of information has been missing from the aesthetic practice setting, yet it benefits those we serve so greatly!

Scope of Practice

A very important factor to consider when offering any nutrition advice is to always work within the scope of practice for your profession. I am an advocate for the protection of the rights of professionals to offer nutrition advice to the public commensurate with the level of their training and expertise. I was part of the team that created a wonderful resource, The Center for Nutrition

Advocacy http://www.nutritionadvocacy.org/, a website designed to help people understand the extent to which they can offer advice based upon the laws in place in their state. In many states, it is actually illegal for someone like me, with my training and education, to offer nutrition advice. This is a result of legislation passed by certain groups who want to monopolize the field of nutrition. Our organization regularly fights unfair legislation to ensure that the public has access to a wide variety of nutrition support that suits their style and needs. It is critical to be aware of these laws and to work within them to ensure that one does not face a lawsuit or charges for offering advice outside of your expertise. You can learn more about the scope of practice of skincare professionals for nutrition in an article I wrote for Skin Inc. entitled, *Is Nutrition an Esthetic No No?* Here I offer some guidelines, with specific examples for skin care professionals who wish to use nutrition as part of their practice. It's important to be a source of credible information to your clients, but not to cross the line by offering medical nutrition therapy advice.

My Mission and Vision

Our mission statement at DermaMed is "to uncover the brilliance that comes from comfort in your own skin." I believe this comfort comes in both emotional and physical forms. It is so rewarding to help people find their confidence again by addressing chronic skin issues. By helping our customers understand the connections between wellness – nutrition, exercise, stress, sleep & mindset – and skin, we can help them better serve the public. I consider it an honor and privilege to serve and educate skincare professionals about wellness, and based on the positive feedback I receive, I think we are filling a much-needed gap for these professionals. I look forward to expanding our training programs so I can reach more students and someday add a wellness coaching program to our company's products offerings. I am passionate about wellness as a crucial tool for skincare professionals to use in practice, and am committed to helping create tools and education to help them offer a truly whole-istic approach to creating healthy skin.

About Ginger Hodulik Downey, MS, CNS

Ginger Hodulik Downey is the co-owner of DermaMed Solutions, a holistic provider of skincare solutions. She is a Clinical Nutritionist, with a BS and MS in Nutrition, as well as a CNS (Certified Nutrition Specialist), for which she completed 1,000 hours of supervised clinical experience.

Her strong science background overlays a ten-year career in the Human Resources field prior to becoming a Nutritionist. In her work as a Nutritionist, Ginger was a key contributor to the GPNS™ program, where she developed nutrition and behavioral modification protocols and programming for a national workplace wellness program. In her current role as the co-owner and Vice President of R&D for DermaMed Solutions, LLC her focus is on researching the latest scientific advances in skincare and incorporating them into DermaMed's holistic approach, which offers superior results due to the "whole person" nature of the protocol recommendations. Ginger lectures, trains and writes blogs and magazine articles educating skincare professionals on nutrition to support the skin.

Ginger's professional affiliations include the American College of Nutrition, The Certification Board for Nutrition Specialists and the Center for Nutrition Advocacy. She serves on the Legislative Outreach Committee for the Certification Board for Nutrition Specialists.

Contact Ginger Today!

Website: http://www.DermaMedSolutions.com

Email: GDowney@DermaMedSolutions.com

Phone: 610-579-6041

Chapter 12

Gratitude

Authored by Ali Shambayati

One winter night in 1981 I woke up to an excruciating pain in the sole of my right foot, the like of which I had never felt before, or since. It was around midnight and 15 below outside. Tehran is known for its fragrant spring blossoms, hot summers, colorful autumns, and cold winters with up to three feet of snow.

I had just spent the previous day working on the usual stuff. As a high-school graduate and an entrepreneur, I would not sit still while waiting for the college entrance exam – a tough proposition for tens of thousands of smart and ambitious students applying to colleges in Iran with only 1 out of 10 getting accepted. In the meantime, I kept working on many different things on the side. Fascinated by machines of all kinds – mechanical, electronic, pneumatic, you name it – I would take them apart in the hope of improving them. Anything that moved by a mechanism piqued my interest. Anything that lit up with LEDs and circuits got my attention. I wanted to know everything about machines and how they worked. So as an 18-year old, I started a business of fixing machines of all types. So much excitement! The sky was the limit. Then everything came to a full stop that night!

By 6 a.m. I had been awake all night with this mysterious, debilitating pain, and a very strange feeling was setting in. Within the course of six hours, my right leg had become paralyzed from the knee down. Was this a dream? It could not be, for the pain was so real I still remember it 37 years later. It was as real as any life-changing experience one can have, and it shaped the course of my life in a way I could have never imagined.

The next day, in utter confusion and unbearable pain, I noticed the same was happening in my left leg. Within 48 hours, I had lost complete control of my right leg, followed by partial paralysis of the left. Crutches were not helpful, as I could not balance myself standing up. I became wheelchair-bound within three days, and my life turned upside down. By that time, I had been awake for three days and three nights from the pain, and no amount of over-the-counter painkillers seemed to work. I checked into a hospital on the third day, and spent the next three weeks undergoing every possible test – from viral infection to neurological disorders, to looking for signs of cancer. What is most memorable in those three weeks is that the pain did not subside, despite being injected with morphine every 8 hours. I remember begging the nurses for more morphine only an hour into a dose, for the pain was so unbearable the effect of the sedative would wear off quickly, but they would refuse, citing the serious addictive nature of the drug.

Three weeks later I was discharged, the hospital claiming they could not find what was wrong with me. Moreover, they said they could no longer help with my pain, which was still in full force, because I had reached the maximum medical (and legal) levels of the drug. I was sent home with no diagnosis, and no relief from the devastating pain. Through desperate inquiries for anything that would provide the slightest improvement, I was introduced to an acupuncturist – a very capable healer as it turned out – trained in China for many years, and one of the pioneers of acupuncture in Iran. During the first session, he inserted some needles in my foot, as expected. Then to my surprise, he placed a small box with electrical wires on the treatment table. He proceeded to attach the wires to the acupuncture needles and turn the knobs on the device. A small pulsation of electricity started flowing through my leg, increasing as he turned the dials on the machine, until it reached a threshold that was too much to tolerate. He then backed it down a bit and left it on. The treatment lasted an hour, and when the needles were removed, the doctor asked me to hold the bed rails and stand up – something I had not done in a month (touching my foot to the ground) because of the unbearable pain. To my surprise, when I finally rested my right foot, the pain was reduced to half – tolerable enough to stand – and while I still could not maintain my balance, at least my foot was on the ground!

I never forgot my reaction to what had just happened: "What was inside that magic box?" (Three decades later, some people refer to TAMA BlueOnyx the same way, calling it the magic box.) This was my first introduction to electrotherapy – a general term that refers to applying electrical energy to the body for the purpose of healing it. Considering my background, my fascination with this device was twofold: first, it was an electrical machine and second, it healed pain! A few more sessions of this magic therapy, and my pain level dropped substantially to where I was finally able to start physical therapy (a long road to recovery indeed, as it took me five years to regain the muscle mass I had lost in just a couple of months).

As the relentless pain finally subsided, I developed a keen sense of appreciation for the complex system of intertwined nerves, muscles, and physiology in general. I understood how demoralizing pain can be through first-hand experience. I could relate to those with chronic pain, and the desperation that ensues. I also understood the limitations of allopathic medicine, relying on opioids as last resort, with minimal or no real benefits, and serious side effects. A sense of purpose was born in me, never mind that I was given six months to live! The mysterious illness which was supposed to take over my whole body did not progress as predicted, and the paralysis remained limited to my legs. Due to my mother's unceasing persistence, I left Iran in 1982 to seek additional medical help. First stop was Germany, where a medical team conducted every possible test, but nothing was found. More medical investigations in America, and still nothing! It was finally concluded that my condition was a form of autoimmune disease that stopped progressing on its own. Why?

Empowered by renewed determination, I continued my life-long passion for understanding how things work. More specifically, I diverted my attention to studying engineering first (learning how to design medical devices), followed by biomedical engineering (learning how these devices interact with the body). The fascination with that magic box never left me, as I would eventually end up devising a similar machine with more capabilities, without the need to use invasive needles. Through a unique energy delivery method which is now known as MetaWave (M2W) at TAMA, the therapy is delivered over the skin surface, and its healing effects not only alleviate pain, they happen to make people look younger!

It took many more years until I finally understood what had happened and why. Thirty years after my life-changing experience, my teacher explained the role of magnetic fields surrounding nerve endings, and taught me how to design the electromagnetic waveforms that allow the body to heal itself. He explained that damaged or severed cells do not feel pain. Instead, the sensation of pain comes from the nerve endings that are intertwined within every part of our body, down to microscopic levels in between cells. Damaged tissue has a distorted electromagnetic field, as its membrane potential changes. This nonuniformity in cellular magnetic field, in turn, signals the nerve endings that an injury has occurred. The nerve then translates the magnetic distortion into a series of impulses that are transmitted to the brain, perceived as pain. Pain, therefore, is an electric impulse acting as a messenger. In the body, everything is an electric impulse, transmitted at different frequencies, thus forming the language of the cells. And every cell has a magnetic field that protects it like a shield. If we can restore that shield through external means, we can help the body regain homeostasis. Welcome to TAMA!

Looking back at three decades of my life and closely examining my experience, I realize that when something we take for granted is taken away, we learn to appreciate it. It may take an extreme personal experience, or that of a loved one, to answer our calling for serving the greater good. We then realize there are many more people who need help, but are left unnoticed until the change occurs within us. If your intention is pure, it paves the way to an open path where obstacles are mysteriously removed as you propel forward. Instead of looking back, you look forward intently. Naysayers and skeptics become a distant memory, as new friends appear along your path. I believe with positive intention, that of helping one another and embracing each other with love, we can change the world we live in. I also believe that expressing appreciation for what you have, and utilizing the talents you are given, is the only way to acknowledge the gifts of life. Remembering who you are, where you came from, and what you have been through, paying tribute to those who have helped you, and reciprocating that by helping others, is one way to express that gratitude.

And as for the business we have started to offer this healing modality to the world, I never forget where these gifts come from!

About Ali Shambayati
Chief Scientist at TAMA Research Corporation

Ali Shambayati is the Chief Scientist at TAMA Research and directs the R&D efforts at the company. Ali has over 30 years of experience in multiple engineering disciplines including clinical and medical instrumentation design, analog and digital circuit design, computer hardware and software development, industrial automation, robotics, and control engineering. In 2011, he co-founded TAMA Research in partnership with Tina Abnoosi. Ali holds a Master's degree in Biomedical Engineering and a Bachelor's degree in Electrical Engineering, as well as 8 patents in various engineering fields. His endeavors in electrotherapy started in the 1980s, as he took on the challenge to develop a more effective technique for treating paralyzed patients through non-invasive electrical stimulation of the skeletal muscles. His research in Biomedical Engineering lead to the development of MetaWave (M2W)™, the patented composite frequency waveforms that are at the heart of TAMA BlueOnyx Smart Microcurrent Systems™. Aside from development of medical therapeutic devices at TAMA,

Ali also conducts educational classes on physiology and microcurrent science.

Contact Ali Today!

Email: ali@tamaresearch.com

Website: https://tamaresearch.com/about/

Phone: (602) 354-8185

Chapter 13

Finding, Maintaining and Keeping a "Younger Me"

Authored by Isabel Dassinger

Throughout my career, my focus has been on understanding aging and its effects on the mental, emotional and physical aspects of health, beauty, and attitude. So well said by Pablo Picasso years ago, "Youth has no age." This would become the mantra for my work in the esthetics industry which has now spanned over 25 years.

I learned from my mentor, Miki Giunta, a pioneer in the concept of internal health and external beauty, to understand this specific correlation and its effects on the four types of health: (1) PHYSICAL (2) MENTAL (3) EMOTIONAL and (4) SPIRITUAL. The quest was to find as many corrective and effective therapies as possible to work on all these levels to hold off the signs of aging and help maintain a youthful appearance.

Cellular health became the obvious answer. In addition to the physical requirements for maintaining and supporting the health and vitality of the cells, I recognized the intrinsic connection of cellular health to mental and emotional conditions. Cellular health was key to overall longevity. As I became a driving force in microdermabrasion, various micro-currents including electroporation and oxygen infusion therapies, I was increasingly drawn to non-invasive technology and techniques as a way to repeatedly and safely stimulate healthy cellular turnover.

Getting Hands-On Experience on How to Meet Client's Needs

After years in the marketing, manufacturing, and consulting end of the business, I decided it was time to understand first-hand what it was like to run my own spa facility. In 2002, I became the owner of the Healing Zone™, an innovative spa and wellness center. It was a true eye opener. We had an interesting clientele looking for beauty and health but, also seeking peace of mind and release from stress, sadness, and emotional turmoil. Healing/wellness therapies were as popular as the beauty/body therapies because they were both needed

An esthetician can become a great confidant to their clients. Sometimes these relationships go on for years. Clients come in needing someone to talk to, to enjoy being pampered and cared for, and to share the stories of their life. As professionals, we are always searching for knowledge to offer and help where we can. I hear from many of my associates how the signs of stress are showing up everywhere so, finding ways to combat stress and maintain a youthful appearance are more important than ever. This chapter of Outstanding Esthetics is my view of what it takes to treat the whole person, both men and women, and achieve that goal.

Understanding the Lymphatic System Effects on Esthetics

I have always studied the environmental effects of life on appearance paying close attention to the prominence of the lymphatic system on esthetic conditions. For several years at the Healing Zone™, we had a doctor who was an Ob/Gyn and a general practitioner. He practiced holistic and Chinese medicine supported by Western medicine learned at Georgetown. He was even a member of Holistic Pediatrics. During those years I learned how to recognize many conditions on multiple levels, from the most severe diseases to general feelings of discomfort and unrest. It seems the lymph system was always a factor. This was often caused by inflammation and stagnation. I saw the effects of a sluggish, compromised lymphatic system on the extracellular matrix and all aspects of health and wellness, and knew that needed to be addressed.

From early on I was taught about the benefits of land and sea plants. Nature had the cures, and amazingly all these plants had been divinely appointed their purpose and benefits. When used as preventative therapies and spa therapies they were able to truly remineralize cells and create balance and harmony within. Even with microdermabrasion, I would think of how a lawn looks that gets mowed too much compared to one that has some height. The evident thickness and richness of the grass reminded me of skin and how important those upper layers are. Keeping them thick and young looking was a challenge to work on, especially when so many therapies lean the other way. Mirroring nature became an easy way for me to evaluate therapies. Also, my goal became to stay natural as best I could through the aging process.

During the 1980's I was the Public Relations Director for AMF, a leading sports and fitness goods company. While there I participated in the introduction of HeavyHands and the concept of adding hand weights to any workout. The general premise was that strengthening the muscles in one focused area would lead to an overall strengthening of muscles throughout the entire body. It is that same realization that blood and lymph flow stimulated in the face will impact the overall wellness of the body. After all, it is an "in and out" life system. The importance of keeping that flow strong and steady shows up in all areas of health.

I once asked an MD friend of mine why there was not more emphasis put on the lymph system in medicine. He said because it was not measurable. However, he said, even so, it is recognized as a life force system within the body where either healthy blood or toxic fluids would travel. Therefore, working to keep those systems clear and fortified was essential to health and beauty.

The Mind Body Connection

Staying physically fit provides a positive reflection that definitely contributes to a healthy mind. When we feel fit, it shows in our face. I have always found it interesting how the expression of joy and happiness can completely uplift a face and sadness and disappointment can turn down a face. I would use essential oils in the treatment room, unless objected to, to provide those energy shifts that I could then translate into treatment results. The careful selection of music, often letting my clients choose, the feel of the sheets and blanket, all the comforts that make someone feel special, relaxed, and peaceful.

This mind body connection was throughout our wellness center, and what we became known for. Amazing result-driven experiences were unique to us, and our passion. That is why it is so important to find your niche in what you want to offer, then do it well, continually gaining knowledge to perfect your skill. Simply put, it is hard work to own and run a spa. The enjoyment comes from seeing your clients leave so much better off than when they arrived.

During the 90's I did Public Relations for the agency IMG Models, and separately for some of their lead models of the day. Here was a situation where these tall, gorgeous, stately "Supermodels," as they were known then, were born beautiful. They were thin, looked great in clothes and had faces advertisers paid hundreds of thousands of dollars to photograph. They were young and often uncomfortable with all the attention they hadn't yet earned. It was fun and almost dreamlike. I saw the physical beauty at its finest but, I also saw how the beauty was conveyed through those ideal faces.

I began to identify beauty as clean, fresh skin, bright, happy eyes, warm, inviting smiles, and a well-balanced, pleasant energy.

Someone was beautiful when you enjoyed being around them. So once again, the importance of a good attitude and emotional balance took precedent as key to aesthetic beauty.

I have always looked at Esthetics as a complete, fully-encompassing art. An art for living, for being and for creating a world where you can shine. In this industry we provide services from head to toe. I truly believe that adding the aspects of internal health or providing guidance and opportunities to explore other healing arts is very important for helping clients connect with their inner selves. This is essential in combating stress and therefore all the other aesthetic face and body conditions caused by stress. Personally, my ideal to stay natural keeps me on the forefront of new and evolving ideals. This is why I created the Younger Me Program. It encompasses all aspects of a full, total body approach.

Here are some of my key components of Outstanding Esthetics.

Stay Balanced

Be in balance and achieve harmony within. Being happy and comfortable with your appearance is a wonderful way to stay in balance. A major, constant pull off that center comes from inflammation. It causes stress, pain, acne and other skin conditions, and robs the skin of essential nutrients. In addition to regular facials and massages, I recommend proper nutrition and key supplements. Younger Me, our anti-inflammatory anti-aging supplement was created to do just that.

Breath/Oxygen/Air

Treatments that stimulate flow, detox the cells, provide essential minerals and clear the channels will make all treatments, both in-the-office and at-home programs successful. Yoga, meditation and other practices that focus on breathing are wonderful for clearing. Even having clients take deep breaths while on the treatment table can have a positive, long-lasting effect.

Equipment

It is the standard in our industry. Equipment can do all things, but moderation is also important. Remember healthy and receptive cells make a big difference in results when using equipment so work on both levels. Our focus has been on microdermabrasion, both suction and compression, face and body power cupping, and other 'current' driven technologies to stimulate the body's response.

Product

We have always supported the use of plants and many other new, powerful ingredients but, in the past few years, we have seen the long-lasting and rejuvenating properties of human growth factors. They have come to redefine age. For skin, for hair and overall youthful appearance, there is nothing that stimulates the youthful factors of the body like these powerful proteins. AQ Skin Solutions is our chosen favorite.

Belief

When you believe in what you are doing it translates. It supports your self-confidence and keeps you going every day.

Stay grounded

Estheticians are blessed to be in this industry. We are surrounded every day by beauty, love and good wishes. I believe that is what makes Esthetics Outstanding.

About Isabel Dassinger

I have always looked at Aesthetics as an element of life that exists on all levels: mental, emotional, physical and spiritual. Through my earlier work in Public Relations working with Supermodels, and Music Icons, and with standout brands such as Redken and AMF Sports & Fitness, and Spa Health Consultants I was given the opportunity to see how beauty and wellness work together.

As President of Diamond Aesthetics now, Healing Zone Aesthetics, and the owner of Healing Zone Spa and Wellness Center, my first-hand look at the industry and its consumers, helped me create Younger Me. This is a program that encompasses my knowledge and experiences in all areas for an effective and easy way for total body beauty and health. Younger Me includes non-invasive equipment, breakthrough anti-aging AQ Skin Solutions, Younger Me Super Supplements, and focused specialty treatments. Woven throughout are philosophies to teach and share and make your own.

Chapter 14

Success Begins in The Mind

Authored by Malinda McHenry

I have been in the beauty industry for 31 years; my career began with desire, focus, and ambition. In fact, these are attributes I know I was born with. They aren't a skill that is learned but an innate sense of one's self. The fact that you are reading this book tells me you probably possess the very same characteristics.

In 1986, I graduated from the College of Coiffure Arts located in Billings, Montana. When I went to school, there was only one 2400-hour program for Cosmetology, Esthetics, and Nails. Thanks to my education I have always been able to support myself and my family. Upon passing my boards and receiving my license, I looked for commission-only employment. I wanted to determine my own worth and set my schedule around my family's needs. I worked at a local salon as a makeup artist and freelance educator for Brocato International and Tressa Colourage through Miller Beauty Co.

I relocated from Montana to the Kansas City area in 1990, and while booth renting at the Perfect Imagery, I was recruited by the accounts executive for Adrien Arpel of NY. I went to work at a local, high-end department store and was suddenly booked nonstop with facials, waxing, and makeovers. Within a year I was promoted to accounts coordinator for seven stores and 12 estheticians. My job was to manage, train new hires, and cover services for the estheticians out sick or on vacation. It was there I met Cathy Berrian who would become my future business partner and best friend. When I first met Cathy, I blurted out I was going to own my own business someday. She joked that she would come work for me and I insisted like fun you will; you will be an owner with me. Cathy is 11 years my senior not that you would know it to look at her. She epitomizes everything we tell our clients to do to look their best. She has amazing skin assessment skills and in my opinion, understands ethnic skin and acne better than anyone.

Adrian Arpel closed in 1996, and I took a job at a local plastic surgeon's office. While there I began using Glymed Plus products and expanded my esthetician skills to a deeper level. After less than a year of office politics, low pay, and a longing to share what I was learning, I approached the distributor for Glymed and offered my services. I discovered that even more than wanting to help my clients feel better about themselves was my passion for sharing my knowledge with other estheticians and cosmetologists.

The distributor had no beauty background and offered to sell me his business for $5000. I only had an American Express card and so convinced this was my excellent opportunity, I took out a cash advance, bought the business, and within a week needed to reorder inventory. I went back to booth renting part time until the distribution grew to need my full-time attention.

In 1997 Cathy and I became Elite Aesthetics Inc., a distribution company, postgraduate training center, and day spa. I was primarily sales and educator for Glymed Plus, Bio-Jouvance, France-Laure, Epilyss, Soundskin, Image Skincare, and Ionithermie. Cathy ran our skincare clinic, managed our retail sales, and salon staff. I did sales and training during the week only working with clients in the evenings and Saturdays. Throughout this time, I submitted articles to various trade journals and was a quoted expert for Day Spa magazine in articles submitted by other writers. I worked an average of nine trade shows a year in sales, and as a speaker for many of the manufacturers we distributed for. I created the training videos for Soundskin Smart Peel Microdermabrasion as well as Candela's Crystal Peel systems.

In 2001, Montana State Board of Cosmetology invited me to train the instructors on peels, microdermabrasion, paraffin facial treatments and sanitation. This was to launch Montana's separation of licenses to include 650 clock hours in esthetics. It was exciting to get to share this with some of my former instructors including the owner of the school I graduated from. At home, I was doing so much training I returned to school at night to obtain my instructor's license. I felt it was the best way to lend credibility to our educational offerings. While training at a local beauty college, I observed that they did not have the staff to keep up with their high demand from future students, limiting enrollment to 14 students a year. I was disappointed they focused only on educating their students from textbook material and focused primarily on the passing of boards.

I approached Cathy about opening a beauty college dedicated to esthetics, and she agreed. Why not build the school we wished we could have attended? We felt it was more important that you had a license to work not just a license to learn. Our school was a gorgeous educational day spa. We had ten equipped facial rooms, two wax rooms, makeup studio, large classrooms, a wet room complete with Vichy shower and hydrotherapy tub. We opened our doors on February 14, 2005, with a charter class of 14. Out of this group, eleven are still practicing in the field of esthetics. In 2009, I collaborated and was featured in nine award-winning educational videos for Aesthetic Video Source. Titles: *Advanced Chemical Peels* Volumes 1-4, *Dry Room Body Treatments* Volumes 1-4, and *The Ultimate Ultrasonic Facials*.

In 2014 we made the difficult choice to sell. Even though we were profitable, our future sustainability was looking low. Our lease was up, there were fewer students graduating high schools, and the industry overall was suffering under the weight of higher administrative costs due to mounting mandatory regulations. We also had a top-notch team of instructors, support staff, and administration staff to consider. As a business owner, you must make decisions that are in the best interest of everyone. They may not be popular decisions or even understood by others, but that is the burden of owning a business.

The Academy of Aesthetic Arts remains my greatest career achievement. We successfully graduated 599 students, had a zero-default rate, a 99 percent graduation rate, 100 percent licensure rate and an 85 percent placement rate. Many of our graduates have gone on to open businesses, and a few have made careers in Hollywood offering esthetics to the stars. We were honored to be a part of others' dreams to pursue a career in esthetics.

In 2012 I formed another small business with my life partner, George Mack. George's background was in construction. Together we opened Bronzed N Beautiful day spa that specializes in organic beauty services including spray tanning. Bronzed N Beautiful has two spray tan studios, two facial rooms, a hair with makeup studio, and a wet room. Together we created a mobile spray tan business for us to work bodybuilding shows and various pageants. George has designed the most amazing extraction fans he calls Spraygon for our spray tan rooms. We currently offer these for other spray tan artists to purchase. Call it a contingency plan, but after closing the school, Cathy has semi-retired and continues to work for us as manager and lead esthetician.

My desire to speak, educate, stay current on market trends, and work with other estheticians is stronger than my need to work behind the chair. But to keep my skills and knowledge growing, I continue to practice on clients ten to fourteen hours a week. I also speak, educate, and attend trade shows whenever I can. I'm currently the territory sales manager in Kansas and Missouri as well as the Director of Schools for Lira Clinical Skincare. Through Lira Clinical Skincare, I get to work with schools to help increase graduate success in the field by offering online education and hands-on training to students.

Today with social media we have access to information good and bad in esthetics. But YOUTUBE can't certify you! There is no substitute for actual learning over virtual learning. To stand out in your field get real, hands-on certification to show your clients. Know your worth and never put your hands on sale. Find a mentor and build a team of colleagues that you can get feedback from. Most importantly if you care about your success, care about the success of others. When you are ready become a mentor and share your knowledge. Everyone has skin and therefore no one's really your competition. Ultimately our goal as estheticians is to make everything beautiful. Be positive, honest, focused and goal driven and you will always stand out as an outstanding esthetician.

About Malinda McHenry

Keeping all things informative, inspirational, and relative for the licensed beauty professional. Malinda McHenry is a practicing cosmetologist, esthetician, instructor, and business owner with a passion for paying it forward. As a former school owner Malinda continues to offer one on one mentoring to school owners, instructors, students, and licensed estheticians with a passion for advanced learning.

Whether you are just embarking on your career or seeking advanced, inspired education that is current and on topic, Malinda's passion is to offer her expertise to others. Many of Malinda's students say that she makes learning fun, easy to comprehend and is deeply knowledgeable about our industry.

Are you ready to be inspired? Whether you are seeking hands on certification or just wish to obtain a deeper education through the convenience of online training, reach out and **Contact Malinda today!**

Contact Malinda Today!

Website: http://www.estheticprofessor.com

Email: malindam@estheticprofessor.com

Phone: 913-940-0461

Twitter: https://twitter.com/MalindaEsthetic

Facebook: https://www.facebook.com/estheticprofessor

LinkedIn: https://www.linkedin.com/in/malinda-mchenry-a053597/

Instagram: https://www.instagram.com/estheticprofessor/?hl=en

Chapter 15

My Journey - The Way We Do Business Has Changed

Authored by Maxine Drake

In the 1980s I carried my massage table uphill in the snow for a halfmile to service clients. I'm kidding! But seriously, whenever I share my story of how I started in the beauty industry I sound like my grandmother who told stories of how life was so hard and the next generations had it so easy. Today, most estheticians are solopreneurs and running a business is far from easy. Yes, doing business today is much different than doing business in the 80s or even 90s, or even the early 2000s, but you still have the same requirements. You must know how to relate to people, and earn their trust before anyone is handing over their money. I did lug my massage table through the streets of Los Angeles to deliver in-home treatments. And yes, I did all of this without GPS or cell phone. I got quite good at mapping out my directions using Rand McNally atlas because if I didn't, I had to stop at a payphone, call my client to figure out where I made the wrong turn. At that time, the mobile spa business model didn't exist, but that is how I started.

What drew me into the beauty industry? We all have a story. I was always fascinated with the energetic level of the human body because I wanted to learn the best forms of relaxation for stress management. I grew up in a rather unbalanced, abusive household and was on a quest to find myself and find inner peace. I was in search of "the truth," whatever that was. I wanted to move far away from any and all negative influences; I didn't believe the limiting things I heard growing up. I knew I could be more than what people told me. I took everything literally, much as a child does, and it has taken years of self-work to break through barriers of self-doubt and confidence issues. I am still a work in progress.

During my journey in LA, I became an LMT, ate vegan, meditated two hours a day, and surrounded myself with incredible, like-minded people in the noisy city of Los Angeles in the 80s when drugs were prevalent, and disco bars were the thing. I was drawn to metaphysics and Buddhism, yoga and meditation on the beach, and running the Santa Monica stairs. I didn't drink alcohol and even went through a period of eating only raw foods. I learned a lot about myself. My true self. My potential. And the impact that I could have on my fellow human beings if I expressed myself fully in the world.

I am a rather quiet individual. I observe. I take time to think. I spend time reflecting. I philosophize. I am drawn to other philanthropists who donate their time, money, and energy to help others. I started writing at an early age and self-expressed through poetry. If you met me at a live workshop, you would surely peg me as an extrovert, as I can be very social, especially doing the things I absolutely love. I love helping others and believe that is why we are on this earth, to share our genius and help one another. It's a simple theory that could have powerful results if all of us practiced it. Every day, we have a choice to tear someone down or make someone's day. Imagine if we all chose the latter.

The 80s was the era of pagers; everyone had a beeper, and this is how we did business. A client or potential client would page us, and we would call them back and hopefully book an appointment. I worked at a fitness center as an aerobic instructor and trainer, and I would convert those clients into massage clients. In those days you didn't run ads in the newspaper, yes, I did say the newspaper. That is how we advertised before Facebook existed and interestingly advertising in the newspaper was a little sketchy for a massage therapist. There was a lot of, well let's just say, extra curricular activities people would include in their massage (if you catch my drift) so I found myself not advertising in the newspaper for that reason. But it didn't mean that obtaining clients back in the eighties was easy. You used the resources on hand, and most of it involved directly connecting with people. We have gotten away from that today, and we need to circle back. When estheticians say to me that they're not successful for lack of resources I say, "Well, become resourceful."

I got into massage therapy because I was fascinated with the human body and I knew that I had the ability to help heal people even though I didn't know how I was doing it. I knew this because people had these experiences on my table and I'd think, *Wow. Okay cool. Something deeper is happening here that's way beyond me, and it's pretty amazing to have this type of an effect on another human being."*

I thirsted for more knowledge within the beauty industry, but I became obsessed with skin for my own reasons of wanting to slow down the aging process and learn how to take better care. I also wanted to make myself more marketable and saw becoming dually licensed as a business opportunity. When I became a spa owner, I sought after potential team members who had dual licenses.

Over the years I moved around a lot, and have lived in the Virgin Islands, Puerto Rico, Florida and currently reside in Hawaii. What do all these places have in common? Lots of sun. So there I was, at the pool one day, lying in the sun totally clueless about sun damage, reading the chapter, "Enemies of the Skin." You remember that chapter in *Milady's Standard Esthetics*? I finished that chapter, closed my book and I never laid by the pool again. I thought, *wow okay my life is about to change.* In the 70s you didn't worry about being in the sun, and nobody wore sunscreen, and very few people even flossed their teeth. I remember lying on tin foil and using baby oil and iodine to get a golden deep tan to give the illusion that I went somewhere cool for a family vacation. I know you're shaking your head right now thinking, *oh my God, I cannot believe an esthetician did this.* And the truth is I had a ton of sun damage from all my years of abuse. The good news is I was able to reverse a lot of the damage with treatments and lifestyle choices.

I landed a job right out of Esthetics School at a department store. This position allowed me to get my feet wet as a new esthetician. I highly recommend working for someone before going off on your own. I have witnessed so many estheticians who had to close their doors because they didn't have a business mind or attitude. Working for someone else showed me how the business works. As a newbie, I was a fanatic about numbers and obsessed with client count and client retention ratios. I wrote out my daily revenues and circled it in bright colors in my appointment book. I wrote thank you cards for every new client and grew my book of business. I loved it. Slow days were a challenge to me and doing the hard work to get new clients in the door, energized me. I loved every part of the process. I know, weird, right? I couldn't wait to open my very own spa. Which is always the next step, right?

I made a ton of mistakes as a spa business owner leading a team of 19. A lot of mistakes. I was still working in the treatment room three days a week while running my business. My consultant coached me to get out of the treatment room, but I didn't want to. I was stubborn. Plus, it was safe in there. I didn't have to face the business end of things. Sound familiar? I didn't understand what it meant to be a leader either. I was following an old school model initially because it's what I learned from my parents who owned businesses. That model just doesn't work anymore and when I had an epiphany and understood I was in the business of growing people things shifted.

Today, I travel teaching business and marketing workshops exclusively for estheticians. I enjoy traveling to those in smaller cities who don't get much education. There's something beautiful about that face-to-face interaction in small groups. I have online programs and run a few groups on social media as a way of giving back.

I believe we can rise above by uniting together and learning the skills we need to learn to have a positive impact in our communities. I envision a world where consumers come to estheticians as part of their culture because everyone knows who we are and everyone understands what we do. My goal is to inspire estheticians through effective leadership, and business knowledge so that we can make that happen. Together.

About Maxine Drake

Maxine Drake is the Chief Inspiration Officer at Maxine Drake Consulting for Spa Professionals and the founder of The Esthetician Business Academy.

Contact Maxine today!

Website: https://maxinedrake.com/

Chapter 16

The Importance of Desire, Dedication, and Support

Authored by Terri A. Wojak

A career can go far with desire, dedication, and support. When asked to write a chapter in Outstanding Esthetic Anthology with leaders in the skin care industry, I was honored. At 15 years old while working in a small salon washing hair, I never thought I would be sitting in this position, writing my story and hoping it would empower future estheticians. As a matter of fact, I didn't even know what an esthetician was, like many people today who ask if we put people to sleep. Four years later, I was still in the beauty industry attending community college to become an accountant while working in one of the most prestigious salon/spas in the suburbs of Chicago. I had no idea what my future was going to hold, and now, when I look back on my aesthetic journey, I think, wow, what a journey this has been.

While on my path to what I could only imagine would be complete boredom, an esthetician in training at the spa asked to give me a facial. I, of course, said yes, thinking it would basically be a face massage. During the treatment, she talked to me about the skin, why I was experiencing breakouts and how to combat them. She then started talking about products that were used and their ingredients which made the nerdy side of me quickly get excited to learn more. An hour and a half later, I called my father with great excitement to tell him I was quitting college and going to become an esthetician. I talked to my father every day; he was the person I trusted more than anyone. He quickly answered, "I don't know what that is, but great – whatever makes you happy." I was surprised he didn't question it or do the usual "dad thing" and start going through pros and cons. I couldn't have been more grateful for his support, as

I thought it might disappoint him. His easy-going response made me quickly realize; there is more to a career than just what you are good at, we all need to take chances and do what makes us happy. Even though it was a snap decision, as soon as I got up from that facial, I knew it would be something I would love.

Enrolling in esthetics school was my next step. While attending school, I quickly became interested in the medical side of esthetics. I heard that estheticians working for plastic surgeons and dermatologists would get to do medical peels, microdermabrasion (which was just becoming available), laser procedures, and even injectables. My goal, much different than today, was to do the most aggressive treatments possible . . . I literally wanted my clients' skin to fall off onto the floor. I thought I could act as a medical professional, like many of the estheticians at that time and even today. I thought the more aggressive the treatment, the better outcome. I tend to think quite the opposite now.

The high-end spa I worked at as a nail technician offered me a job as an esthetician. The job started with an intense three-month training program. That training took me from "I can rub someone's face with lotion" to "I am able and ready to make people look and feel better." I had an amazing instructor, Fabienne Lindholm, who was tough but always went above and beyond to ensure her students knew everything. She inspired me to go to the next level and got me more interested in education. I thought over and over about going back to school to be an educator, but I was very shy and thought I would never have the courage to do it. Instead, I worked hard to become the spa director at one of the locations and got the position almost a year after I started. Soon after becoming spa director, the company developed a skin care line and asked me to train the estheticians at other locations. I was still terrified to talk to groups of people, but decided to take the challenge. My first training experience was horrifying! I had to train top estheticians at the flagship location in downtown Chicago, I was 23 at the time, and these women had been in the industry 20 to 30 years each. They looked at me with great disappointment, and one said, "Who are you to teach us about skin care?" I didn't think I could be more afraid to talk in front of a group of people, (until now, when I speak to large rooms full of dermatologists and plastic surgeons). I ran to the bathroom to hold in my tears and put on my strong face. It was one of the hardest things I had to do at the time for my career, but I did it, and following the training, the estheticians thanked me and truly appreciated it.

During the next five years, I worked hard building a full clientele, eventually managing the spa, and training as needed. I couldn't have been happier. I was then approached by two of my co-workers that were leaving to open a medical spa, and they asked me to manage it. I had another big decision to make, as I was doing great, it seemed stupid to leave to start all over again. It was scary, but I decided to take the jump to gain more knowledge of the medical esthetics world. The business didn't survive very long, due to unforeseen circumstances with the owners, which made me upset and regretful for leaving a place I was so comfortable in. I then turned my negative thinking into positive, and realized at the very least it gave me experience in the medical field and the ability to branch out. I ended up working at a few salons and spas, doing lasers part time for a gynecology office, and even renting my own space before finding my way back to medical esthetics full time. I attended a seminar that a prominent plastic surgeon, Dr. Steven Dayan, was giving for estheticians to learn more about their roles in a medical practice.

A few months later, I saw an ad for a skin care manager in a medical office, it was very vague, but I decided to apply. Low and behold, the interview was for Dr. Dayan's office. At that point, I was working 32 hours a week at a local salon with a perfect schedule including weekends off and doing very well financially. The job offered about half the pay of what I was making in the spa, but I knew I had to do it since this prestigious company offered an opportunity to grow. The position at Dr. Dayan's office involved revamping the spa department, working with clinical research, assisting in the clinic, and treating clients. It was a tough decision, but I chose to expand my career instead of staying where it was comfortable.

My first week at the office, Dr. Dayan and I discussed how there was no training for estheticians who want to work in a medical setting. He looked at me and said, "Why don't you put something together?" I laughed thinking to myself, he must be joking. His straight face made me quickly realized he was serious. Having a mentor that is open-minded and supportive is what gave me the confidence to try something I had never done before. After several conversations about how we could make this happen (by the way, Dr. Dayan's motto is Make it Happen), I spent the next six weeks trying to build the best one day course for "Esthetics in a Medical Setting" as possible. I shadowed Dr. Dayan and stayed up all hours of the night reading his medical books to gain as much information as possible. As I was observing and learning, it finally clicked, estheticians should not be performing medical treatments. Our positions in the medical world are about expanding on what the physician can do, retaining patients, and making people feel better about themselves.

I have become passionate about teaching and developing materials for esthetics in a medical setting. It is important for estheticians to know about medical treatments so that they can treat clients safely and effectively before, during, and after medical procedures. There is a gray line between what estheticians are allowed to do and what they are not. I strongly believe that estheticians need advanced training to work in the medical field, it is important to enhance and maintain what the physician has accomplished without over-stepping boundaries. The bridge between skin care and cosmetic medicine is becoming more clear as physicians are starting to see the real benefit of having estheticians and the importance of incorporating a holistic approach.

The aesthetics industry continues to evolve, and I am extremely happy to be a part of it. I feel very lucky to have a career I love; life is too short to spend time doing something you're not excited about. My passion for aesthetics comes from making people feel better about themselves in one way or another. When I am teaching, it makes me happy to bring eager students to the next level of their careers. When I am treating clients, it is the look on their faces when I help them feel more confident about themselves that brings me joy.

I started out saying a career can go far with desire, dedication, and support. Desire: if there is something you want, go after it. No matter how hard or impossible it seems, if you want it bad enough, you can accomplish it. Dedication: keep pushing yourself to meet your goals. It's not always easy, but in the end, it will be worth it. Support: surround yourself with people that believe in you. Look for a company that will support your ultimate goal, and it will be much easier to succeed.

About Terri A. Wojak LE, NCEA

Terri Wojak is a highly sought-after aesthetic professional with over 20 years of experience in the industry. She is a respected authority on skin care in a medical setting, education, and business development on multiple levels. Wojak has built 50 individual courses based on skin care in a medical setting. More than 70 articles by Wojak have appeared in a multitude of industry magazines, and her previously published book, Mastering Medical Esthetics debuted in 2009 through CCM publishing, and her latest publication, Aesthetics Exposed through Allured was recently a bestseller in the skin care category on Amazon. Always a highly requested speaker at skin care seminars, medical conferences, trade shows, and international aesthetic symposiums, it is difficult to quantify the number of people she inspires. Terri has trained over 7,000 estheticians and medical professionals on the importance of building the bridge between skin care and cosmetic medicine, ultimately helping medical providers and patients alike.

Chapter 17

Esthetics is a Business

Authored by Beth Kenerson

Sometimes we pursue the things we know we want, and sometimes the best things in life come to us. The esthetics industry fits this statement like a glove. As a girl, teen, and young adult, I had no idea there was this thing called an esthetics license. All I knew was that I loved ingredients, aromas, textures, and possibilities – bath, skin, and aromatherapy enchanted me.

My very first W-2 job was at Lotions and Potions, a teensy little store in my local suburban mall owned by a woman named Shirley and her two adult daughters. Shirley was no fool; she saw the opportunity to hire an individual who not only loved her tiny brand but would also turn her paycheck back over each month in retail sales!

Lotions and Potions was jam packed from floor to ceiling with salts, balms, spritzes, and my very favorite, a custom blending bar, its crown jewel. Shirley taught me to count back change, conduct inventory, keep a subtle eye on the sticky-fingered customer and the power of merchandising, all before I had a driver's license. Thirty years later, my 40-something self would love to thank her for the phenomenal example she set for the 15-year-old me.

Fast forward to 1999 when I discovered that you could go to school to learn all the things about product, skin, and ingredients – I felt like I had hit the jackpot! I had already finished a four-year degree and had no desire to sit in a cubicle, so it seemed like a dream come true. At the time, I was an international flight attendant, a tough but flexible workflow which was interrupted by 9/11. The massive furloughs allowed me to take a leave and enroll at a Chicago Pivot Point, which launched my 15 years (and counting), in this industry.

Post Pivot Point, I did what many new estheticians do; I went to work in a mixed service salon setting. As is often the case for new estheticians, it did not work. It was decent experience but not for me, so I set off on my own, sharing space in a trendy Chicago neighborhood loft with an individual who taught me several more lessons. These were unpleasant, ugly lessons about working with people who say they like and respect you, but in fact, carry closely the goal of hurting you. I can be hard headed but not in these cases – lesson taken and learned thank you very much.

Sheepishly pulling my ill-prepared shingle back inside, I started searching for that job – the one with the great manufacturer, the name recognition, the cool exposure, and benefits. I had no idea that this was not so much an esthetician gig as it was business side management, an education, and sales position. Once I understood the difference, doors started opening. I spent almost five years as an educator and regional education manager with a former major brand, then moved on to another education position with an international brand, all the while spending every spare moment in the treatment room at a gorgeous Chicago spa I was incredibly sad to leave after nine years.

More experience in the retail channel followed the corporate jobs – the type of experience that is unmatched for broad industry scope and forward thinking. It wasn't exactly *fun*, but it was incredibly valuable. When I was finally ready, I rehung my shingle. I had set aside several years to decide what I really wanted, understood what worked, and far more importantly, what does *not* work, which is critical.

Let me share some things I have learned:

YOU CAN DO ANYTHING YOU WANT TO DO.

One of the very best things about the professional esthetics industry is the endless options available to you and the complete absence of boundaries. You can switch gears when and if you're ready, no explanation needed. Don't like facials? Fine? Love providing Brazilians? Stock your shelves with body and post care, heat your pots and don't look back. Hate waxing? Fine, refer it out and concentrate on smart aging microcurrent. Creating a niche is one of the smartest things you can do for your career. Build a brand and nurture it 24/7.

ESTHETICS SCHOOL IS OVER, LET THE LEARNING BEGIN!

I get it, this is not necessarily what you're dying to hear, especially if you're new, but it's the truth. Education is grossly undervalued, particularly in the wake of social media. Esthetics school, no matter how costly the tuition, is just the tip of the iceberg, a tiny ripple in an ocean of what's to come, yet too many people think their work is done when their hours are finished.

Many of us are fortunate to have had a really positive esthetics training experience. On the other hand, many of us did not, and that's ok too because once the state hands over a license to yield a fan brush, the true education gets started, which is true for *everyone*.

LISTEN MORE THAN YOU TALK, PARTICULARLY ON SOCIAL MEDIA, BUT GET INVOLVED.

Or in this day and age, perhaps it would be more appropriate to *read* more than you respond. It takes time, you'll feel like your head is bursting, it's frustrating, but keep reading and watching. Eventually, it will pan out – the silt falls away, and the gold will appear in the pan. Equally important, don't believe everything you read online, who's to say the respondent is any smarter than you!

LEARN THE ROPES and SPEAK UP FOR YOURSELF.

You have a voice, and it counts. It can be easy to get overwhelmed, and that's ok. Whether you're wading into the industry fresh or switching from a busy plastic surgeon's office to corneotherapy, the learning curve can actually be enjoyable if you don't push it or rush it.

This industry is governed by a lot of rules – rules that affect not only your income but the validity of your licensure. Learn these rules. Ignorance might be bliss somewhere, but it's no excuse for flying by the seat of your pants in the treatment room. Google the life out of what you don't know, then quadruple check it with the powers that be. The answers *do* exist.

YOU WORK FOR YOURSELF…EVEN IF YOU DON'T WORK FOR YOURSELF.

Perhaps your *preference* is to work for a corporation or a large, luxury chain. Maybe managing a busy staff at the leading spa in your city is your dream job. There are so many amazing opportunities for estheticians. Keep in mind that even when someone else signs your check, *you* and only *you* own your image, your behaviors, and your reputation. Take a spa in which there are 20 rooms including 12 skincare and eight massage therapy. Out of those 12 skin therapy rooms, make no mistake, whether it's in Manhattan NY or Manhattan KS, there will be three or four pros that are jam packed weeks out, with zero room for new clients and a waiting list that can't be cracked. The pros behind *those* doors, new or veteran, have built, for all intents and purposes, a business within a business. Practice client education and retailing until it's second nature.

Practice extreme sanitation. Work toward becoming a beacon of leadership in your work environment, people WILL notice.

PRACTICE APPRECIATION.

Set complaints aside. The easiest thing in the world is to give in to group complaining, to pull your shoe off and throw it into the ring so you can co-commiserate. Stop it. Bad energy breeds bad energy, positive, grateful energy breeds light. Other people notice your radiance, will be attracted to your energy and bit by bit, great things begin to happen.

DON'T WORRY ABOUT THE COMPETITION – RUN YOUR OWN RACE.

There's no other way to get things done except to keep your eyes on whatever your own personal goals are for the career that lies in front of *you*.

Competition: n. a contest, a rivalry, a competition is a situation in which two or more people or groups are trying to get something which not everyone can have.

Personally, I'm in the *competition, what competition?* camp. In any industry, but particularly those heavily marked by entrepreneurship, it's easy to spend more time looking from side to side to see what others are up to than to hoe your own row. Stop it. Be your own thought leader. I have the extraordinary pleasure to have more than a few six figure esthetician colleagues (they're not as rare as you may think) in my circle with whom I would happily work side by side. Each one of them is far too busy doing their own thing to worry about the other, let alone waste time on thoughts of competition. Quite the contrary, we regularly share what product, resources, and equipment work, what doesn't and *why*!

The reality is, there's exactly nothing going on around you that you can't create for yourself.

Definitions belong to the definers, not the defined.

Toni Morrison

ESTHETICS IS A BUSINESS.

Repeat after me. Esthetics is a business. Not a sideshow, not a hobby, not a sorority. The pros who make it the longest, who are making a comfortable living and continue to grow year after year understand that an issue of Inc. magazine is equally important as a class on advanced peels. Placing as much emphasis on administrative and business priorities as new enzymes is the smartest move you can make for longevity.

Some may call it cliché, but *fail to plan, plan to fail* is an entrepreneurial truth, so watch the trends and learn by reading major retail journals. One of the worst sinking feelings, personally, and certainly professionally, is not being prepared. Sometimes it's something as simple as discovering you're short a hot towel to conclude your service, but sometimes it's much bigger.

Check your professional temperature regularly; taking the long view is rarely if ever a fail. The esthetics industry will continue to be a profitable, thriving environment for those who choose to grow *with* it verses in spite of it.

About Beth Kenerson

Beth is a veteran esthetics professional and director of the Esthetician Success Lab™, a one of a kind content development company that caters to the licensed skincare and beauty industries.

Beth appreciates that your key strengths (and most of your time and energy), may lie in the treatment room. She also understands that your demands for professionalism and polish don't end there - you need communication that reflects your treatment room excellence.

Backed by years of advanced esthetics instruction, protocol and theory development, hands on practical experience and a passion for writing, a rare pro niche has finally been filled by Beth.

Esthetician Success Lab™ successfully marries esthetics wisdom with the ideal words that describe exactly what you do - an accomplishment only a colleague who has spent years in the treatment room can successfully deliver.

Contact Beth Today!

Email: beth@estheticiansuccesslab.com

Website: http://www.estheticiansuccesslab.com

Instagram: https://www.instagram.com/estheticiansuccesslab/

Facebook: https://www.facebook.com/estheticiansuccesslab

Chapter 18

It Is Never Too Late.

Authored by Margaret Tomaszewicz

August 20, 2013, changed everything. It was the day my husband and I dropped off my only daughter at college. Please do not get me wrong; I was extremely happy for her. She was about to attend the school of her dreams to become the person she wanted to be since she was five years old. Someone had asked her when she was five what she wanted to be and she answered, "I want to have my own film studio."

There she was carrying her things, meeting her roommate, checking out her dorm room and in less than twenty minutes of arrival she turned to us and said, "Ok I've got this, you can go now." What? You don't want me to make your bed, help you put your clothes in the closet, make sure you have everything you need? I guess not…I received a one arm hug, and a look that said, "please do not embarrass me, Mom."

The next morning things were never the same for me. I had just lost my most important daily role as Mother. It took some adjusting! There definitely is such a thing as empty nest syndrome!

Don't feel bad for me though because I lived in Santa Monica, California where the average temperature was 70 degrees, with no snow or pollution. Health food stores and yoga studios were a walking distance from home. I had a wonderful husband, two adorable dogs, and a good job.

At that time I was the most requested esthetician at a well-known Day Spa in Santa Monica. I had practically no commute, and I could arrange my own working hours! I had a long list of steady clients that were happy to see me on a regular basis, and many of them became my friends.

I had been working there for twenty-five years though, and for me, the pleasure of working for someone else was definitely gone. I still loved seeing my clients each month and helping them with their skin care needs, but after 25 years I was simply bored.

My daughter was in college, and my husband and I had typical empty-nest conversations. My dogs were still excited to see me coming home every day, but since my clients were also my friends, I was all talked out by the end of the day. I began to think there must be more to life.

Let me give you some background about myself. I escaped to California from communist Poland in 1980. I was 19 years old and barely spoke English. I arrived with two suitcases and $10 in my wallet. But I was in America, the land of opportunity, and I was young and ready to learn!

After doing a couple of waitressing and babysitting jobs that helped me get a car and an apartment, I realized I needed to learn a good trade. Unable to support myself through a four-year college, I went to check out Santa Monica City College. And there it was, the Cosmetology Department, with young people full of artistic talents and dreams of becoming famous.

So I enrolled, and it was a wonderful experience. I made a lot of friends, and one of them introduced me to her neighbor who became my future husband. We all had so much fun, and I became a pretty good hairdresser. At that time skin care was not my primary interest, but I did have a wonderful skin care teacher.

After finishing school and passing the state board exam, I went to work as an apprentice in a big hair salon. It took only two weeks before I realized, how much I hated being there! The noise, loud music, the smell of chemicals and being on my feet for eight to ten hours a day, running from one client to another to check on the hair color or perm (yes we did those then) was not something I was loving.

And then one evening after coming home exhausted I thought of my skin care teacher. I went to her for advice. She suggested I go to the newly opened Dermal Institute in Marina del Rey, run by the now famous Jane Wurwand.

The moment I met Jane I knew that I wanted to be like her. She was fun and so full of knowledge. Her school was calming, relaxing and uplifting to my soul. I quit my hairdressing job, enrolled in the Dermal Institute and never looked back. I finally found my calling!

Learning directly from Jane was incredible. She had only been in the United States a couple of years. She came from England and brought a much needed European style of skin care to America. She now runs the International Dermal Institute and her Dermalogica skin care line is available worldwide. She is an inspiration to all of us!

After finishing the course, I got a job in a small skin care salon owned by no other than Dr. Howard Murad. OMG! At the time there was no Murad Skin Care, although daily we were testing the mysterious substance in plain plastic bottles he called glycolic acid.

If I only knew then that in the future his innovation would change skin care, I would have never left his side! I learned a lot from this kind, funny, and wonderful doctor.

The next job I got was the start of my 25-year adventure with the well-known day spa. I was only the third esthetician to work there. We started developing new treatments and boy did we had fun. We went to classes, tried many different products, and we were constantly learning new things. We got busy fairly quickly and soon moved to a bigger location, and the spa opened many more locations over the years. During those 25 years I gave birth to my daughter, and because I wanted to spend time raising her, I declined a manager position in the corporate office.

So let's go back to the beginning of this chapter when my daughter left for college. What will I do now? I was 53 years old. The spa I worked at for so long was no longer a small, family business, and I was no longer enjoying it.

I had been asked many times why I did not open my own business. At that time I didn't want the responsibility of going out on my own, working for someone else was all I knew.

How would I start? I did not have any business training. I decided to contact two friends, one was a massage therapist and the other an esthetician, to see if they'd like to start something with me. We were all past fifty years old, but not in our hearts! I was feeling like a kid again and wanted to discover new things.

Together we rented space in Salon Republic in Santa Monica. I slowly cut down my schedule at the spa, and within four months I gave my resignation so I could spend all of my time building our dream business. We named it European Skin Care and Massage Studio.

Within a couple of years, we all went our separate ways but remained friends. I was on my own now, not an easy undertaking. Keeping my vision in mind kept me going. I was now doing it all: treatments, scheduling, laundry, advertising and sweeping the floors! I did hire a person to redo my brand, make a new website and get it on the first page of Google and Yelp.

One day a client asked me if I would be interested in participating in the Golden Globes gifting suites. It was an intriguing idea; an event like that could bring me a lot of exposure. But what do I have to gift at the Golden Globe? It came to me in the middle of the night! What if I develop a skin care line? Yes, that's what I'll do! The next morning I emailed my client and told her to count me in.

I only had six months to create my skin care line, and I didn't know the first thing about getting started! I hit the internet and researched everything I could find out about making skin care products. I knew I wanted it to be organic, no animal testing, affordable, and most important results driven. I had worked with a lot of different skin care lines over the years, and now it was time to put my knowledge to work. For the next six months, my poor husband did not get a home-cooked meal, and he even started doing his own laundry.

Before too long though, WODA European Natural Skin Care was sitting on the shelf in my studio. I did the Golden Globes gifting suites, the Grammys, and the Academy Awards. I had great support from my husband, my friends, and a great team of people that surrounded me. I could not have done it without them.

So, what's next? My skin care line is doing well. It's available on Amazon. I was voted one of the five best facialists in Santa Monica, and I am privileged to share my story with you in this book. I had never thought about telling of my journey as an esthetician, but I think it is important to share our stories.

Many of us are working by ourselves or just starting out. We are sometimes filled with fear or frustration. Believe me; I was there many, many times. There were days I thought maybe I would not make it. But then I would read about someone that overcame difficulties and succeeded. That gave me the inspiration to keep working.

I'd especially like to reach out to baby boomers. If you think you are too old to start something new, you are wrong. You have wisdom and experience that no school can teach. If you fail once or twice, get up and start over again. Go for it! Surround yourself with like-minded people, separate yourself from naysayers who tell you that you cannot do it.

Please close your eyes and picture yourself in one year. Where would you like to be? Now write it down. Thoughts become words and words become reality. Believe me; it is never too late!

Best wishes to you all!

About Margaret Tomaszewicz

A native of Warsaw Poland, Margaret Tomaszewicz came to Southern California in the early 80s. Polish women for centuries recognized a need for great quality skin care.

Polish cosmetics were highly recognized by European women. In the USA, the skin care revolution was just beginning. With a passion for skin care, Margaret was privileged to be on the ground floor of this development.

She worked in the first skin care salon of Dr. Murad learning from him about skin care health. She fondly remembers working with Dr. Murad's while he was creating his products still in their developmental stage.

Training with the founder of Demalogica Jane Wurwand, a United Kingdom therapist, Margaret saw a vision of bringing European knowledge of skin care to the United States.

Then it came the concept of the Day Spas lead by Burke Williams. Margaret worked with its owners on the ground floor developing services, training therapists and later having input in the Burke William skin care line.

After 26 years, Margaret used all of her knowledge to start her own European Skin Care Studio in Santa Monica, bringing the best skin care services to her Studio, Margaret carried the tradition of her European roots by offering Luxury at affordable prices.

Her established and loyal following including celebrity clients, loves the combination of European touch combined with forward thinking and newest technologies.

In 2016, Margaret used all of her acquired skills, knowledge and experience to begin developing her new skin care line-Woda, which translated from Polish means water. Made with natural and organic ingredients, the skin care products are created with a deep understanding of every ingredient and its effects of the health on the skin.

From dry, sensitive, mature, acne prone, sun damaged-all skin type problems are addressed in the Woda Skin Care Line. Every woman can find an effective and simple answer to help the skin become the healthiest that it could be. Her products are now available on her website wodaskincare.com and on Amazon.com

Margaret is committed to giving back to the community by supporting the American Cancer Society and its feel good/look good program. She is also a certified oncology aesthetician and a member of the International Society of Oncology Aesthetics.

At her studio Margaret offers personalized oncology facials for people living with cancer.

In addition, Margaret also partnered with the organization One Tree Planted. For every product sold the organization plants a tree in California.

Margaret is always searching, learning, and traveling the world to find new treatments, technological breakthroughs and natural products to help her clients look their best.

She resides in Santa Monica with her husband, daughter and two dogs.

Contact Margaret Today!

Email: europeanskinandmassagestudio@gmail.com

Phone: 424-2799771

Chapter 19

Your Money Mindset and Success

Authored by Shelley Hancock

I don't recall my parents worrying about money when I was young. I'm the fourth child to come along, and my Dad had pretty much created a successful business by the time I was born. But what I do recall is my Mother saying "we didn't have a pot to pee in or a window to throw it out of." She was referring to their lean years when the two of them first got married and started having kids. I wasn't around for those years, so I think that not living through the lean years helped me with my money mindset. I watched my Dad go out and purchase things without even investigating which brand was best or what would be the most economical. As a kid, it seemed like he would just point and pay.

I know many of you heard your parents say, "money doesn't grow on trees." I think maybe I believed that money did grow on trees because of the way my Dad approached the subject. We weren't overly wealthy, but my Dad didn't seem to have issues around money or at least he hid them well, which set me up to have a similar mindset.

As I purchased my first skin care business in July of 1990, I wasn't scared about money. I was scared of failure, but it had nothing to do with money. I don't recall sitting around worrying about how I was going to pay next month's rent, or the business loan, or purchase the products I needed to do my work. I do remember though the excitement about digging in to create a successful esthetic business and I believe that the excitement was the key to why I did just that… create a successful business.

The other day I found my taxes from my first year in business. I made $49,000 that first year. Not bad for a 29-year-old kid with no business background and only having my Esthetic license for 18 months. I don't know if it was youth, or naiveté, or my money mindset, but worrying about money was not something I did in those first years in business. When I sold that business in 2005, it was bringing in close to a quarter of a million dollars. Had I been fearful of money, that growth could never have happened.

Let's talk about your money mindset. Where is your mind when you want to purchase a new piece of equipment for your business, or try some new advertising, or venture out into another avenue in the industry? Are you excited or scared? I hear the word scared quite often when consulting with my fellow Estheticians. I encourage you to take that word out of your vocabulary. Be excited, not scared. Be curious, be inquisitive, be interested, be eager, but do not be afraid.

I recently read the following statement in a book called You are a Badass. (Great book, by the way, I highly recommend reading it!) Here's a quote from the author, "It was about no longer being the kind of person who takes what she can get, and finally becoming the kind of person who creates exactly what she wants." Now that's what I'm talking about. Jump in and create the life you want rather than sitting on the sidelines accepting what's dropped into your lap.

She goes on to talk about how money is currency and currency is energy. I truly believe this. Those of you who know me know that I speak about energy quite often. Good energy or bad energy, whichever you exude, you'll bring more of it to you. If you walk around grumpy, you will get more to be grumpy about. If you spend the day worrying about money, you will most definitely get more money issues to worry about. Like attracts like. You get what you think and talk about. It's that simple.

Okay, it's that simple, but it's not that easy. We are hardwired for the negative. Have you noticed when there's a possibility of something going wrong (it hasn't happened yet, it's just a possibility) your mind goes right to the worst-case scenario? We are hardwired this way for protection, but it doesn't serve us well, does it? We can waste a ton of energy thinking about something that may never occur. Wouldn't it be more beneficial to use that energy thinking and talking about how you would like the outcome to be? Remember that what you think about and talk about comes about.

How many times do you hear yourself say, "I don't have enough money for that or I can't afford to do that?" Too often, right? That's what I thought. So change the verbiage in your mind and also what you say out loud. Think and talk about abundance, not lack of it.

Here's one of the ways we cut ourselves off from creating the fabulous life we want. You say you want something, but then in the next breath, you negate it with your words. How many times have you said something similar to this? "I want to go on a vacation," and then in the very next breath, you say, "Oh, but there's not enough money, and I can't get the time off of work, the kids have too many projects and what would I do with the dogs?" So you've stated your dream, and then you've immediately negated it. You made excuses as to why you can't go on that vacation. Do you want the vacation or do you want to keep making excuses? You can't have both. You can either have the dreams you want or the excuses for why you do not have them, but you can't have both. That's powerful! Think about it.

Let's use a business example. An opportunity drops in your lap. Whatever this opportunity is will take you out of your comfort zone. You can feel the fear creeping up your spine already. This opportunity could also be a possibility for some major growth for your business. That feels good when you think about it that way. So you spend the next few days wavering back and forth between running away as fast as you can or jumping in with both feet. Remember, you can't have both. Which do you want? You can make excuses about why it wouldn't work out, how you are just too afraid, or how much work it would be, and then you'd feel justified for not jumping in, Or, you can talk about how great the outcome is going to be, how it will change your life, and then get excited about it, and jump in full steam ahead.

Every time I've purchased a new piece of equipment for my business I've never spent any time whatsoever thinking or worrying about how I am going to make my investment back. I don't worry if my clients will be able to afford the treatment. I don't worry if they will like the treatment. I don't worry if they'll book for another treatment or a series of treatments. I could go on and on with worry thoughts! Instead, I spend my energy excited about how my clients are going to feel after they've experienced this treatment, excited about how they are going tell their friends about what they've just experienced, excited about how they will book for a series of treatments and pay in full right then and there. Can you feel the difference?

Here is a fact. I have always paid off my equipment in less than a month. Most times it was less than a week. I'm not making this up; it's the truth. The reason for this is my mindset. Failure does not enter my mind for one minute. I have a childlike excitement about my new equipment that draws people in. People are drawn to that energy. They want to be around it. They want some of it. So if you exude it, they want what you've got, even so much as to pay to be around you (get treatments by you) and that creates success.

Your beliefs about money hold the key to your financial success. If you truly believe that you can have whatever you desire and then go for it, you will get it. Believe you can and you will.

About Shelley Hancock

Shelley Hancock, (a.k.a 'The Gadget Gal'), is one of the most trusted esthetic advisors of our time and Founder of Shelley Hancock Consulting, an organization dedicated to helping estheticians increase their profits. After owning a successful skin care center for 29 years, Hancock expanded her focus so she could provide a deeper level of service to fellow estheticians. Through hands-on training, workshops and private consultations, she has now connected 1000s of beauty business owners with esthetic equipment that attracts a higher level client and helps build a more successful practice. "Most retailers think the relationship ends with purchase," explains Hancock. "I view it as just the beginning".

When she's not teaching, training, coaching or working with clients, you will find her recording her radio program for Voice America.

Contact Shelley Today!

Website: http://www.ShelleyHancock.com

Email: contactme@shelleyhancock.com

Notes

Made in the USA
Columbia, SC
20 January 2022